To Linda

Modular Origami with
Super Nobu Unit

Thank you for your interest!
I wish you all the best!

Nobuko Okabe

Nobuko Okabe
OKABE NOBUKO
岡部 伸子

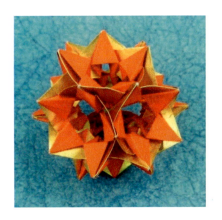

Modular Origami with Super Nobu Unit

Super simple, super versatile unit that can
be assembled in many different ways

Copyright © 2017 by Nobuko Okabe
All rights reserved

No part of this publication may be copied or reproduced by
any means without written permission of the author

ISBN-13: 978-1974053551
ISBN-10: 1974053555

To My Family,

Masami, Yuko, Shoko, Ryohei and Helene

Contents

Acknowledgments ... 7
Preface ... 9
Origami Symbols in This Book ... 18
Materials ... 20

1. Super Nobu Unit ... 21
   1.1 Folding the Unit ... 22
   1.2 Characteristics of the Unit ... 23
   1.3 Mass Production of the Unit ... 27

2. Assemblies ... 29
   2.1 Aligned Edge Assembly ... 30
      Single Width Band with Zigzag Edge ... 30
      Double Width Band with Zigzag Edge ... 32
      Sheet ... 34
      Alternative Connection - Choosing Which Side's Pocket to Use ... 35
      Forming a Ring with Zigzag Edge Band - Regular Ring and Mobius Ring ... 39
      Straight Edge Band ... 41
      Alternative Connection in Straight Edge Band ... 43
      Connecting Two Straight Edge Bands Perpendicularly ... 45
   2.2 Angled Edge Assembly ... 50
      Polygons (Single Layer Rings) ... 50
      Polyhedrons ... 55
         Dodecahedron 1 ... 55
         Dodecahedron 2 ... 58
      Polyhedrons with Larger Number of Units ... 59
      Polyhedrons with Smaller Number of Units - Limit of Angles ... 60
      Tube (Layered Rings) ... 62
   2.3 Combined Assembly ... 67
      Pendant ... 67
      Net Type Modular ... 67
      Net Formed by Aligned Edge Assembly ... 68
      Net Formed by Angled Edge Assembly - Formation of Torus ... 74
   2.4 Other Assemblies and Miscellaneous Subjects ... 88
      Assembling Units of Different Sizes ... 88
      Horizontally Joined Rings ... 90
      Locking Units of Different Sizes on Both Sides ... 91
      Bringing Units Closer to Form Joints on Both Sides ... 95
      Disassembling - Limit of the Joint ... 97

ACKNOWLEDGMENTS

First of all, I would like to express my special thanks to Ms. Tomoko Fuse for giving me a strong motivation to materialize this book. Ms. Fuse has been one of the biggest inspirations of my origami life, as she must be to many other origami lovers around the world. Without her interest in my module and her sincere, encouraging words to put all my works together, I would not have thought of making them into a book. She even gave my module a new and very special name, "Super Nobu Unit," which is an amazing honor. It is such a brilliant name that I still feel a little awkward using it myself. But here it is and I will treasure it all my life.

I also would like to thank Wendy Zeichner, the president of OrigamiUSA, for finding a way to publish my work as a book, by introducing me to JC Nolan, and for help with editing my English. I thank JC for his kindness and guiding me through the publication process.

Thank you to my friend Deanna Kwan, the organizer of our local origami group, for spending enormous amounts of time to proofread my diagrams and texts. Deanna has proofread some of my diagrams in the past also, but this was far longer and had many different types of drawings. I appreciate Deanna being there to help me all the way to the end.

I also would like to thank two of my good origami friends Yongquan (YQ) Lu, a former president of OrigaMIT, and Keiko Kawabe, a member of OrigaMIT, for spending time to proofread my early, very rough draft and giving me many valuable suggestions. I thank YQ for helping me edit the final draft too.

I thank my family, especially my daughter Yuko, a professional illustrator, for lending me her computer programs as well as her technical help, and my husband Masami for helping me solve problems with the computer that arose every so often.

Thank you to all my friends for their support and encouraging words.

Preface

It still feels a little surreal to me that I am really publishing an origami book of my own. I have always enjoyed the works of so many talented origami artists and admired the amount of effort they put into publishing their works. After experiencing how much work, time, energy and focus it took to complete my small book, I now see all those authors with renewed respect.

This is a book of just one unit. It is a very simple unit; so simple it may look unsophisticated and insignificant. But it is a very versatile unit; so versatile it may seem wild and almost unruly.

The story of this book starts at the 2016 OrigamiUSA convention in New York City when Ms. Tomoko Fuse who was a Special Guest of the Convention stopped by the table where I was folding and chatting with my friends. She asked us what we were folding. As many of us know, despite her worldwide fame, she is a very nice, fun and friendly lady. We were very excited to have a chance to talk with her, and as she sat down with us, we happily showed her this unit and models that can be made with it. After folding some units and assembling them, she stopped her hands and said, "Sugoi!" which means "terrific" in Japanese. I was very happy she seemed to like my unit and the models, but thought it was just her social compliment to us locals. But she went on, "I've never seen a unit like this before. It's very unique and interesting. It should have your name on it. How about 'Super Nobu Unit'?" Tomoko Fuse, one of the most respected and admired modular origami artists in the world, was personally naming my model? It was really an incredible honor. But I was so surprised I could not keep up with her words and asked her if she was serious. I even grabbed her shoulder and asked her again. After all, this was a unit that had received very little attention for more than 7 years even though I had published, taught and exhibited it at several conventions In New York and elsewhere. But Fuse Sensei was calm and serious. She suggested that I sort out all the assembly options of this unit and put all the works together in one article.

So I started the work after the Convention, although I was not really sure where it would take me.

On the short list of the origami models I have designed, this module is one of the first ones. My idea was simple: A unit needs to have insertion flaps, pockets and a locking mechanism. Later on, I started designing units that use only a part of the sheet for joint formation and save the remaining part for decoration and variations. But I think Super Nobu Unit is one that is as simple and primitive as you can get with those bare basic functions.

It took me some time to explore the possibilities of the many different types of assemblies this unit offers and embrace its almost wild versatility. Having so many options for the angles and orientation of units was making the discussion complicated but also very interesting! As I assembled models and drew diagrams, other new ideas and possibilities came up and things kept evolving. But I finally reached a point where I said to myself "I conclude this book here." I can only hope everything I have presented is clearly written and drawn. I am open to your suggestions and questions, as I consider this book an experiment. Since this unit can be joined with other units in almost any way you want, there are many more possible shapes you can form.

I hope you enjoy this book. Let me know if you come up with some interesting ideas.

Nobuko Okabe

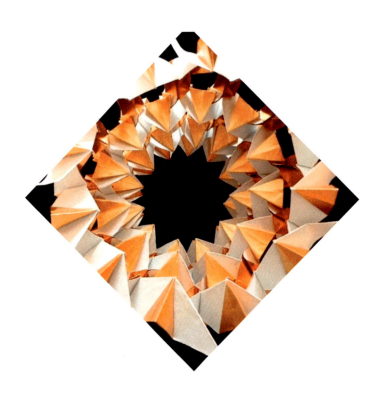

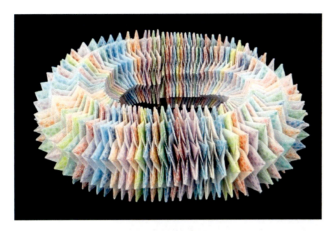

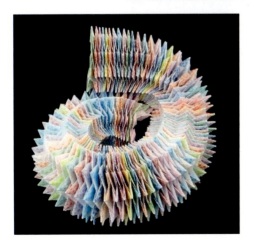

Tube (layered rings) (3 in. x 3 in. squares) (pages 62-66)

Regular and Mobius rings with single width zigzag band (1.5 in x 1.5 in. squares) (pages 30-31, 39)

Pendant (1.5 in x 1.5 in. squares) (page 67)

Regular (left) and Mobius rings with double width zigzag edge bands (1.5 in. x 1.5 in. squares) (pages 32-33, 40)

Sheet (3 in. x 3 in. squares) (page 34)

Double double-ring (1.5 in. x 1.5 in. squares) (pages 45-49)

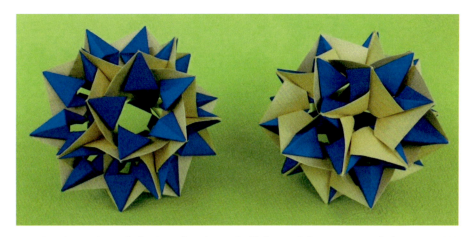

Dodecahedron 1 and dodecahedron 2 (3 in. x 3 in. squares) (pages 55-58)

Truncated icosahedron (1.5 in. x 1.5 in. squares) (pages 55-59)

12-ring torus (1.5 in. x 1.5 in. squares) (pages 74-86)

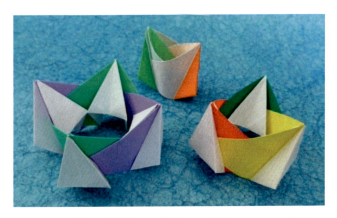

2-, 3- and 4-unit rings (3 in. x 3 in. squares) (pages 50-54)

5-, 6- and 7-unit rings (3 in. x 3 in. squares) (pages 50-54)

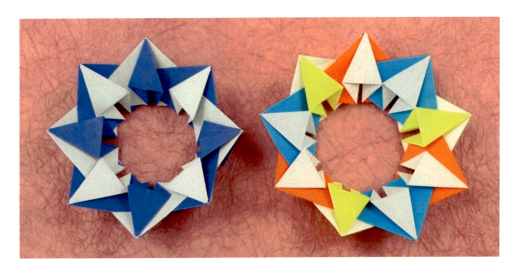

8- and 9-unit rings (3 in. x 3 in. squares) (pages 50-54)

10-unit rings (3 in. x 3 in. squares) (pages 50-54)

11- and 12-unit rings (3 in. x 3 in. squares) (pages 50-54)

Horizontally joined 10-unit rings (3 in. x 3 in. squares) (page 90)

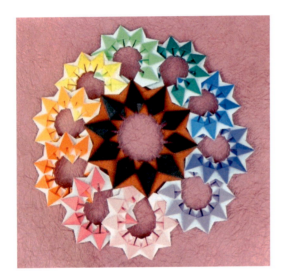
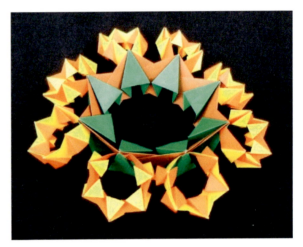
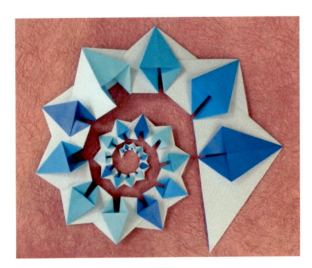

Examples of models formed with units of different sizes (pages 88-94)

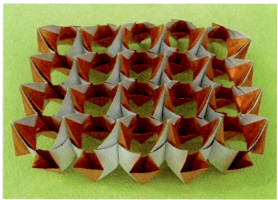

Net with 4-unit rings and 4-sided holes (top and bottom views)
(2.5 in. x 2.5 in. squares) (pages 68-71)

Tall torus (2.5 in. x 2.5 in. squares) (page 87)

ORIGAMI SYMBOLS IN THIS BOOK

LINES

- - - - - -   Valley fold

-·-·-·-·-·-   Mountain fold

————   Crease line

· · · · · · · · ·   Edge of paper or a part of a line hidden under other layer

ARROWS AND OTHER SYMBOLS

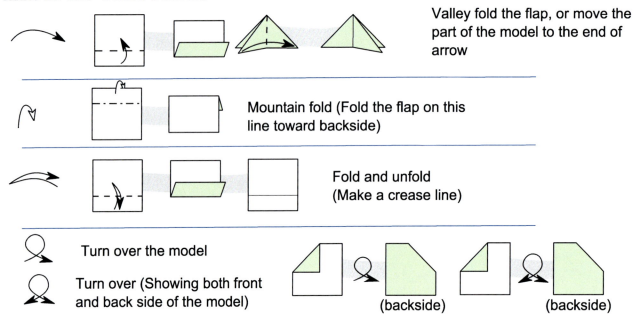

Valley fold the flap, or move the part of the model to the end of arrow

Mountain fold (Fold the flap on this line toward backside)

Fold and unfold (Make a crease line)

Turn over the model

Turn over (Showing both front and back side of the model)

(backside)   (backside)

Rotate the model (Note that the arrows show the direction of the rotation)

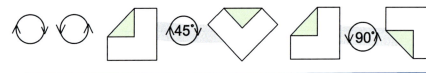

Enlarged

Shrunken

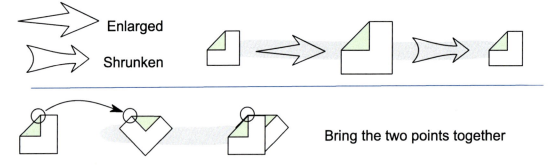

Bring the two points together

 Separate the two layers

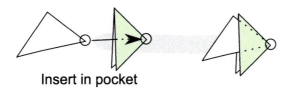

Insert in pocket

 Push this point

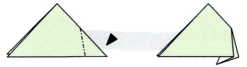

Inside reverse fold

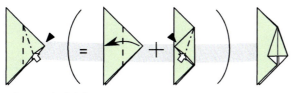

Squash fold

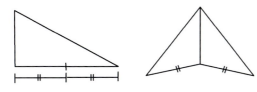 Equal lengths

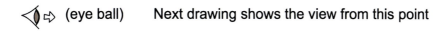 (eye ball)   Next drawing shows the view from this point

MATERIALS

PAPER TYPE

Almost any type of paper can be used for the models in this book unless it is too soft to form a reasonable crease. Choice of paper type depends on the model you are planning to make and the effect you are looking for. Regular origami paper, duo paper, foil paper, duo paper with foil on one side and copy paper of different weights are used for the models in this book. Since both sides of paper are visible in a finished model, duo paper offers the best color effects. Foil makes finished models stiffer and helps them maintain their shapes while regular paper makes the model more flexible. For example, a tube made with regular paper stretches very well and moves freely while a tube made with foil paper maintains its shape better and does not stretch or move as freely.

PAPER SIZE

Most models in this book are made with squares that range from 1.5 in. x 1.5 in. to 3 in. x 3 in. Most of the 3D models stay in shape better when paper of these sizes are used although some start loosing their shapes after a while because of their flexibility and the weight of paper. Since these units and their assemblies are very simple, you can use smaller paper too. For example, rings made with 1 in. x 1 in. (or even smaller) squares can be worn on your fingers. 3D models made with larger paper tend to be more flexible but do not maintain their shapes very well as you can see in the truncated icosahedron made with 4.25 in. x 4.25 in. squares (page 59), but it is fun to play with as it stretches well in all directions!

So, the choice of paper type and size really depends on what you are planning to achieve. I hope you experiment and find your own way to enjoy this module.

1. SUPER NOBU UNIT

1.1 Folding the Unit

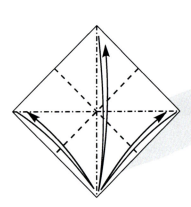

1. Crease to form a preliminary base. Unfold.

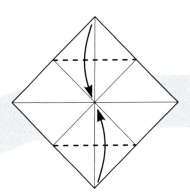

2. Fold two opposite corners to the center.

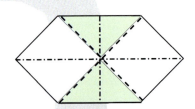

3. Form mountain and valley creases as indicated to obtain the shape shown in 3a - 4.

3a.

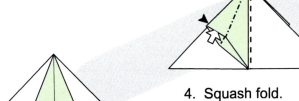

4. Squash fold.
(This is a pre-crease for assembly.)
Repeat on the back.

5. Unfold the pocket flap to step 4.
Repeat on the back.

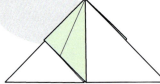

6. Super Nobu Unit completed.

★ To produce 4 or more pieces of the same unit from one sheet of square paper, you can use the method described on page 27.

1.2 Characteristics of the Unit

1. This is a very simple unit with two pocket flaps, one on each side, and two insertion tips. Each of the two pocket flaps can be moved to either side and therefore works as two independent pockets (Fig.1), So there are two insertion tips and four pockets on each unit.

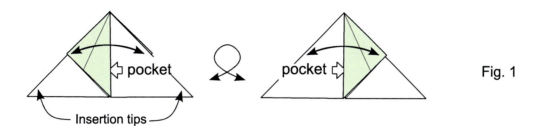

Fig. 1

2. Each of these four pockets can accept insertion tips of other units from different angles within 45 degrees as shown below. Also, other units can be oriented in the same way as the first unit (Fig 2a, 2b), or placed upside down (Fig. 2c, 2d).

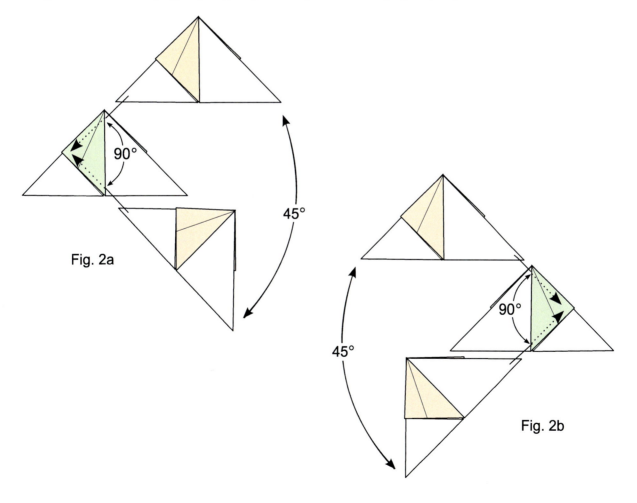

Fig. 2a

Fig. 2b

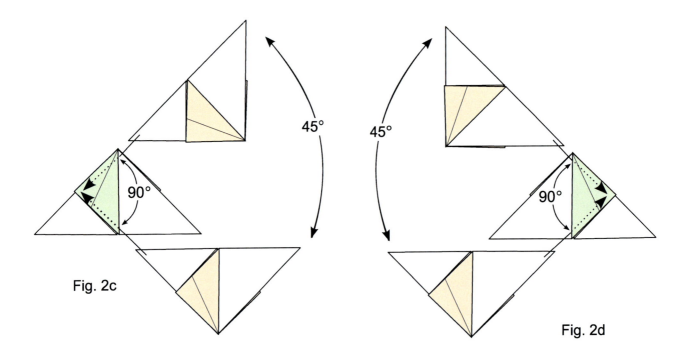

Fig. 2c

Fig. 2d

3. Once an insertion tip is inserted and the insertion angle is determined, the pocket flap is folded to the right and the insertion tip is locked in place. By squash-folding the pocket flap, the insertion tip inside the pocket is folded again (i.e. double locked) and thus the joint is reinforced. This locking mechanism is the same with all the models described in this book.

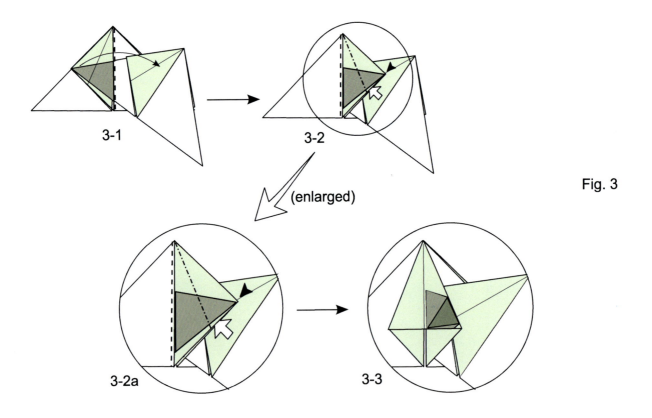

Fig. 3

4. Many of finished models are highly flexible because of the mobility of each unit.

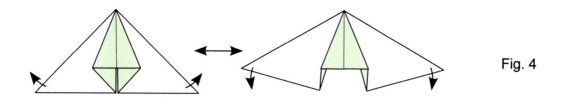

Fig. 4

5. This unit can also be squeezed as shown when smaller angles are necessary in assembly,

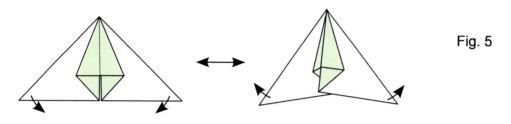

Fig. 5

★★★
All the characteristics of the unit allow each unit to connect to other units in different ways with strong joints to form many different types of 2D and 3D modular models. These modular models include flat bands, sheets, rings, polyhedrons, layered rings/tubes, nets, torus (donut shape), etc. and also combinations of those geometric objects.

In this book, I will discuss the assembly methods in the following categories.

1) Aligned Edge Assemblies where edges of an insertion tip and a pocket flap are aligned. Two dimensional modular models such as bands and sheets can be formed by these assemblies. As mentioned in pages 23-24, any two units can be oriented in the same way or upside down, resulting in more variations. Also, these bands and sheets can be formed into a ring or tube by connecting one end or edge to the other end or edge.

2) Angled Edge Assemblies where two units are connected with certain angles, usually angled by using certain reference points.
Polygons (rings and wreaths), polyhedrons, layered rings/tubes and torus can be formed by this method. Most models formed by this method are very flexible and stretchable.

3) Combination of the two assemblies 1) and 2).

4) Other types of assemblies and miscellaneous subjects including disassembling (limit of the joint).

1.3 Mass Production of the Units

You can produce 4 X n units of the same color pattern from one sheet of square paper to save a little time.

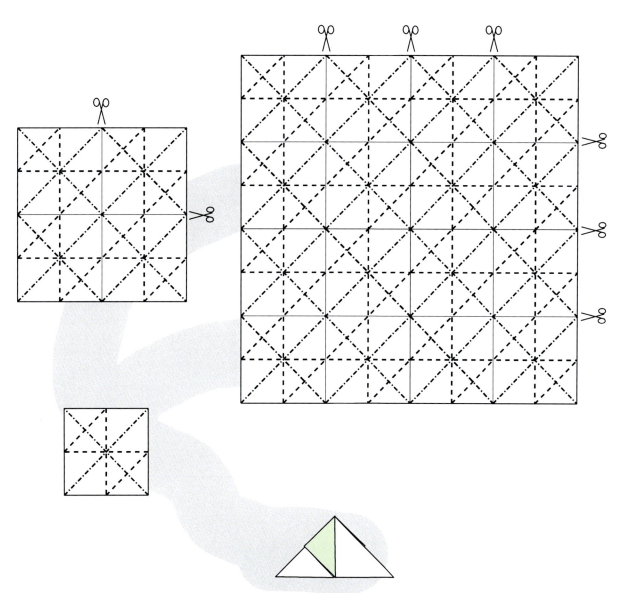

Unit same as the one obtained in step 4 on page 22.

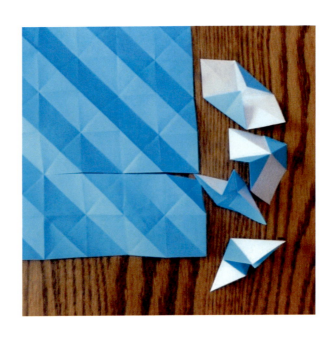

2. ASSEMBLIES

2.1 Aligned Edge Assembly

Single Width Band with Zigzag Edge

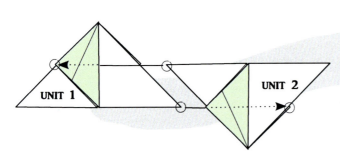

1. Insert a tip of UNIT 2 into a pocket of UNIT 1. Also insert a tip of UNIT 1 into a pocket of UNIT 2 on the back.

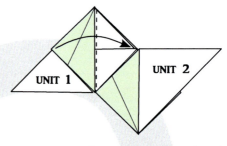

2. Fold the pocket flap of UNIT 1 to the right.

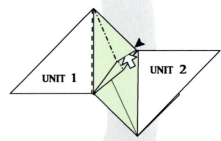

3. Squash-fold the pocket flap.

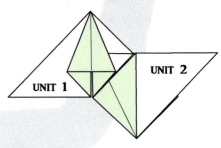

4. Repeat steps 2 to 3 on the other side on UNIT 2.

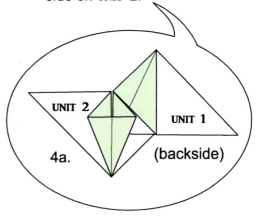

4a. (backside)

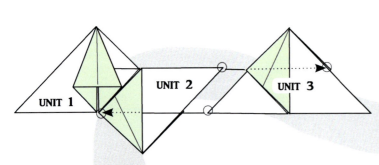

5. Add the third unit in the same manner.

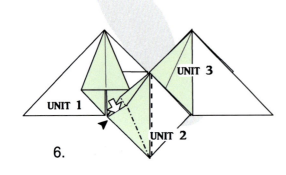

6.

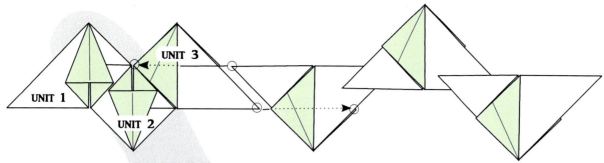

7. Add additional units in the same manner.

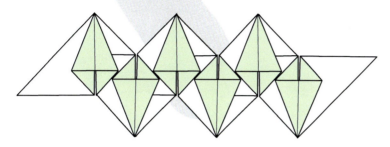

8. Six units are connected.
Add more units to form a band of desired length.

NOTE: This single width band is very stretchable.

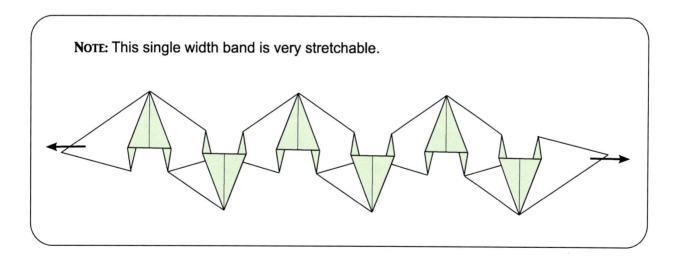

Double Width Band with Zigzag Edge

You can make the band wider by adding units on both sides of a single width band. Double width bands are more stable (i.e. less stretchy) and more decorative too.

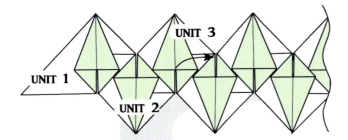

1. Form a single width band of any length. Then, unfold the pocket flap of UNIT 3 to the right.

(turn over)

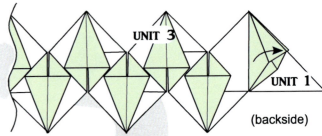

2. Also, unfold the pocket flap of UNIT 1 on the backside.

(turn over)

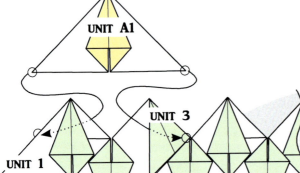

3. Insert a tip of UNIT A1 into the pocket of UNIT 3. Also insert the other tip of UNIT A1 into a pocket of UNIT 1 on the backside.

NOTE: Here, units for second rows are called "UNIT A" (A1, A2, A3,--) to make distinction although they are the same units as the ones in the first band.

NOTE: UNIT As' pocket flaps are squash-folded on both sides because they are not used for this assembly.

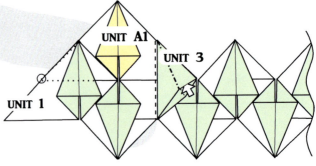

4. Squash-fold the pocket flaps of UNIT 3 (front side) and UNIT 1 (backside).

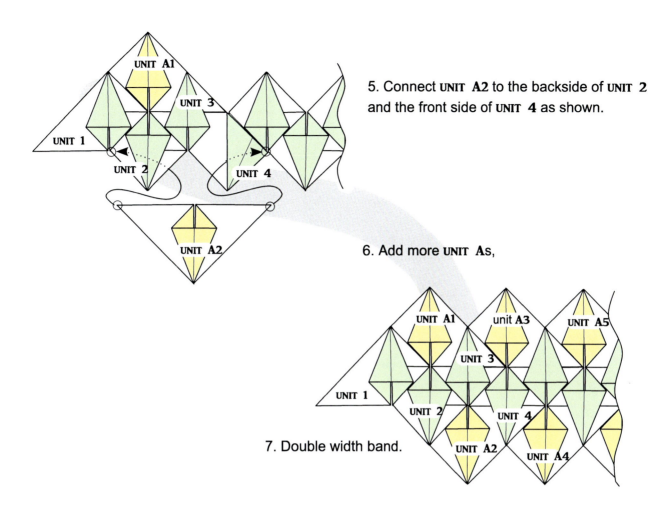

5. Connect UNIT A2 to the backside of UNIT 2 and the front side of UNIT 4 as shown.

6. Add more UNIT As,

7. Double width band.

Double width band (2 in. x 2 in. squares)

Sheet

You can add more units on each side of the band to make it wider and form a sheet.

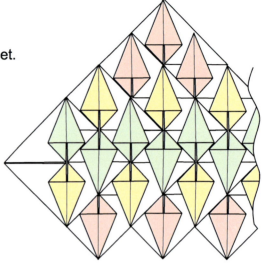

Sheet (3 in. x 3 in. squares)

ALTERNATIVE CONNECTION – CHOOSING WHICH SIDE'S POCKET TO USE

Single Width Band

In the diagrams on pages 30-34, the insertion tips are inserted on certain sides so that all pockets are used evenly. I call it a "regular connection" method.
However, as mentioned in the Unit section, this unit has the same pocket flaps on both sides and they can be moved to right or left, so an insertion tip can be inserted in the pocket on the other side of the unit too. I call it an "alternative connection" method.

These two different connection methods are compared below in a three-unit assembly.
"Regular connection" is shown in box **I** and "alternative connection" is shown in box **II**.
(Insertion flaps of UNIT 2 below as well as that of UNIT 4 on the next page are shaded to make the difference between the two connection methods more visible.)

I. Regular Connection

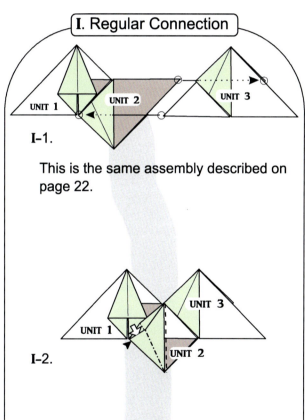

I-1.

This is the same assembly described on page 22.

I-2.

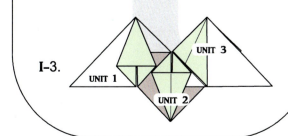

I-3.

II. Alternative Connection

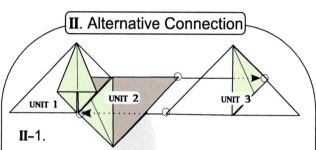

II-1.

In order to insert the tip of UNIT 2 into the front pocket of UNIT 3, front pocket flap of UNIT 3 needs to be moved to right.
Pocket flap of UNIT 2 on the backside already has the tip of UNIT 1 inserted and squash-folded, so it needs to be unfolded to accept the tip of UNIT 3.

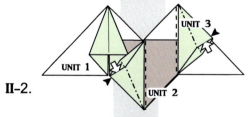

II-2.

Front pocket of UNIT 3 is squash-folded to lock the inserted tip of UNIT 2. Front pocket of UNIT 2 is not used here but it is also squash-folded to obtain a consistent look.

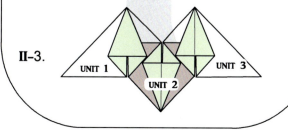

II-3.

The next unit (UNIT 4) can be added to either side of UNIT 3 in both I-3 and II-3.

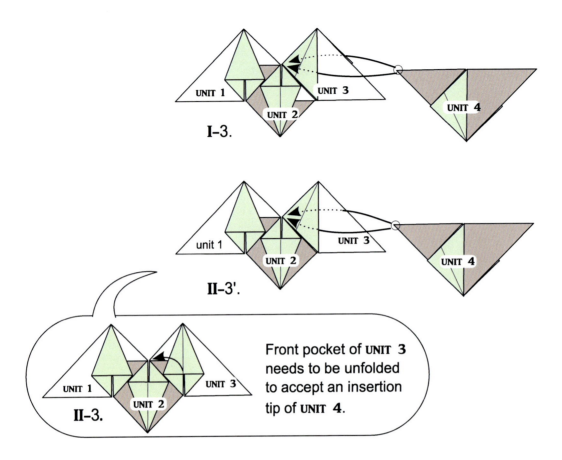

Front pocket of UNIT 3 needs to be unfolded to accept an insertion tip of UNIT 4.

★★★
This choice can be made with every additional unit in all assemblies of 2D models including double or wider width bands and sheets.

When all insertion tips have the same color, it does not affect the appearance of the final model. But, because both sides of paper is visible in this unit, when you assemble units that have different color patterns, you need to decide which pocket to use to obtain a certain pattern.

Double Width Band

Tips of second row units can be inserted from either side of first row units too. This is the same when you add more rows to form a sheet.

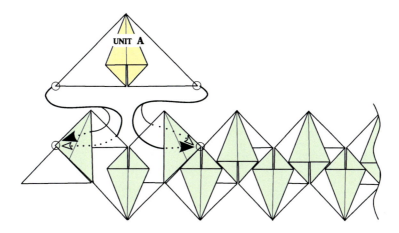

Examples

Some Examples of single and double width bands formed by using pockets on different sides are shown below and on the next page.

Combining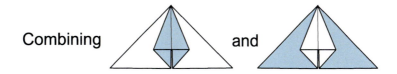

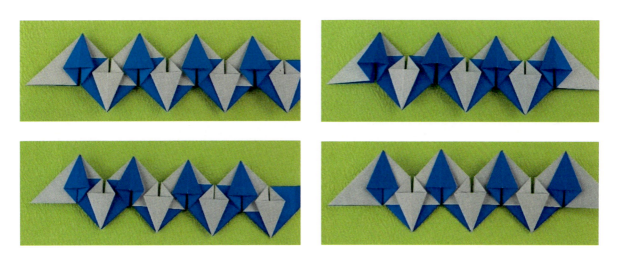

Single width bands

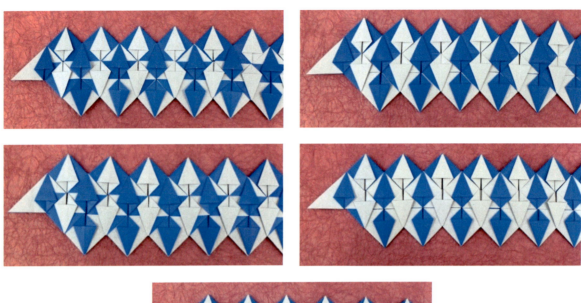

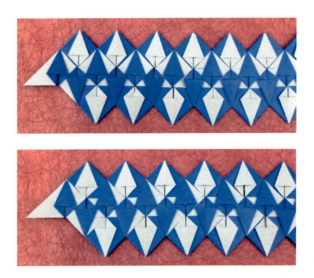

Double width bands

Forming a Ring with Zigzag Edge Band
– Regular Ring and Mobius Ring

Rings with Single Width Band

If you form this band with an even number of units and connect the last unit to the first unit, you will have a regular ring. When you form a band with an odd number of units and connect the last unit to the first unit by twisting the band, you will have a Mobius ring.
(See photo on page 12.)

REGULAR RING

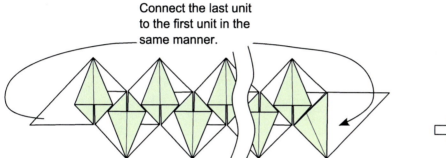

Connect the last unit to the first unit in the same manner.

⇨ **REGULAR RING**

Assemble an even number of units to form a band.
Then connect the last unit and the first unit.

MOBIUS RING

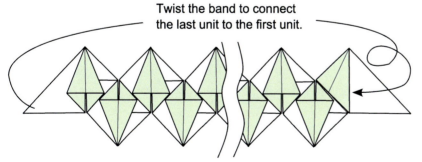

Twist the band to connect the last unit to the first unit.

⇨ **MOBIUS RING**

Assemble an odd number (11 or more is recommended.) of units to form a band.
Then twist the band to turn the last unit upside down and connect it to the first unit.

Rings with Double Width Band

Double width bands also can form both regular and Mobius rings.
(See photo on page 12.)

> NOTE: The drawings below show the structure of the bands before two ends are connected, but when you actually form double width rings, it is recommended to form a ring of single width band of desired size first and then add units to widen the band.

REGULAR RING

You need 2n units.

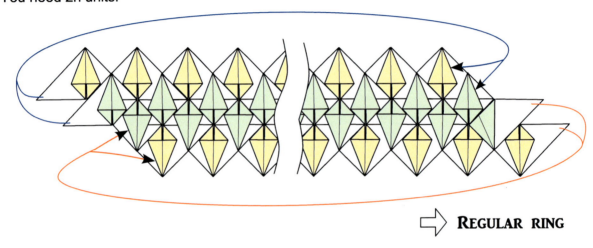

⇨ REGULAR RING

MOBIUS RING

You need 2x(2n +1) units. For double width Mobius ring, n>7 is recommended.

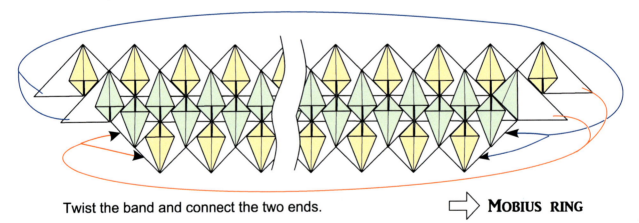

Twist the band and connect the two ends.   ⇨ MOBIUS RING

> NOTE: You can form rings with wider bands. When a band is wider, you need larger number of units to form a Mobius ring.

Straight Edge Band

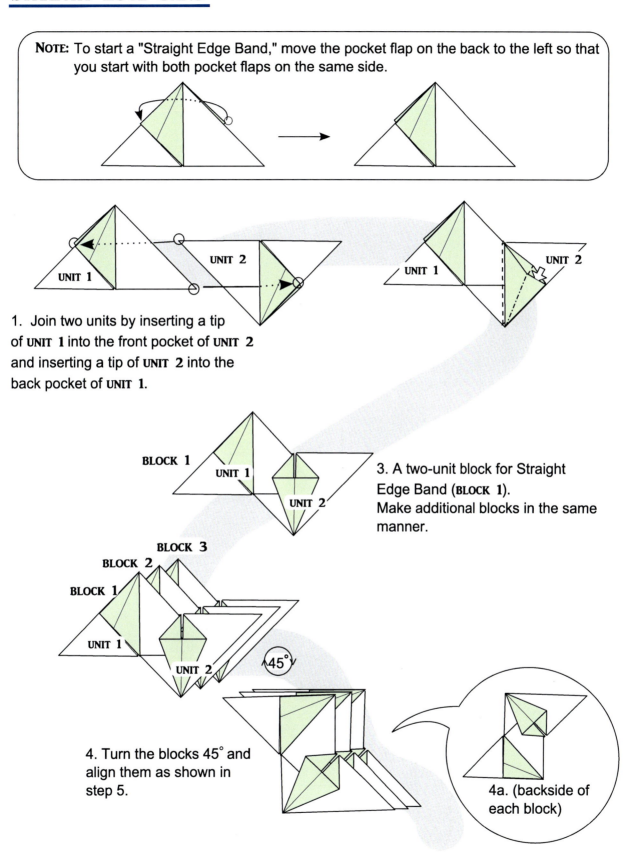

NOTE: To start a "Straight Edge Band," move the pocket flap on the back to the left so that you start with both pocket flaps on the same side.

1. Join two units by inserting a tip of UNIT 1 into the front pocket of UNIT 2 and inserting a tip of UNIT 2 into the back pocket of UNIT 1.

3. A two-unit block for Straight Edge Band (BLOCK 1). Make additional blocks in the same manner.

4. Turn the blocks 45° and align them as shown in step 5.

4a. (backside of each block)

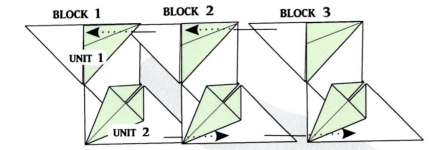

5. Insert tips as shown.

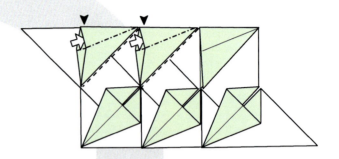

6. Squash-fold the pockets. Repeat on the back.

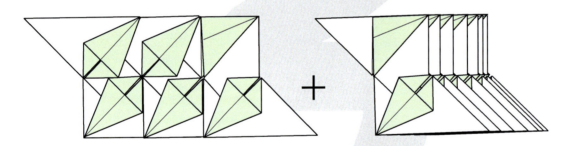

7. Add more blocks in the same manner to form a straight edge band of desired length.

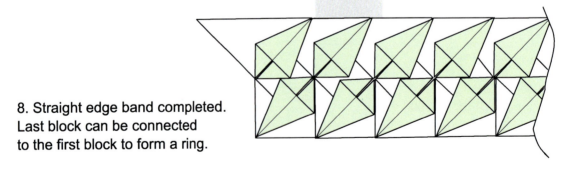

8. Straight edge band completed. Last block can be connected to the first block to form a ring.

Alternative Connection in Straight Edge Band

As discussed in Zigzag Edge Band, insertion tips can be inserted in the pockets on either side of units when you form a Straight Edge Band too. Squash-folded pocket flaps need to be unfolded to accept an insertion tip and squash-folded again after another tip is inserted.

As mentioned in Zigzag Edge Band, when all inserting tips have the same color, it does not affect the color pattern of finished band, but when you assemble units with different color patterns, you will obtain a little different result depending on how you arrange units.
(See examples on the next page.)

For each additional block, there are four different ways to connect.
(Insertion tips of each block is colored differently to make the difference more visible.)

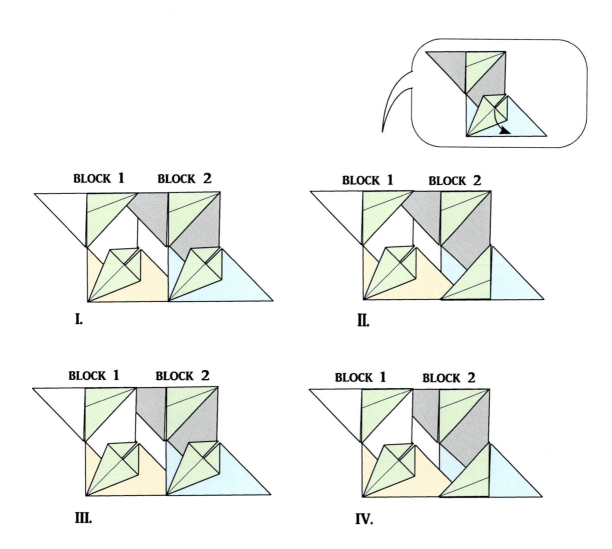

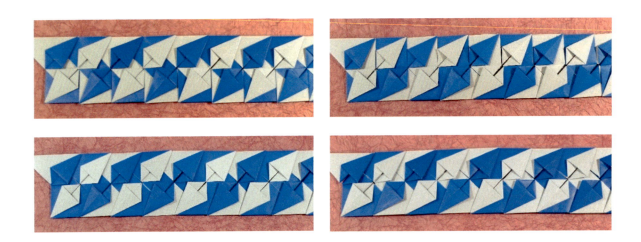

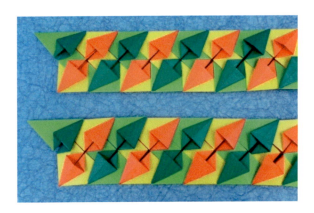

Patterns obtained by using pockets on different sides in straight edge bands

Perpendicularly connected straight edge bands

Connecting Two Straight Edge Bands Perpendicularly

It is possible to connect two straight edge bands perpendicularly.

In the diagrams here, the units that are used to connect the two bands are named UNIT A (BAND 1), UNIT B (BAND 2) and UNIT C (BAND 2).
Note that both UNIT B and UNIT C have to be connected to UNIT A because of the orientation of units in straight edge bands.

1. Prepare two straight edge bands of desired length (BAND 1 and BAND 2) as described on pages 41-42.

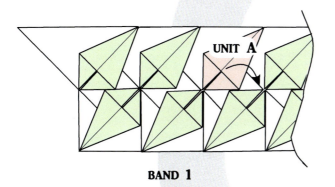

BAND 1

2. Select a unit (UNIT A) to be connected to BAND 2 and unfold the pocket flap of UNIT A.

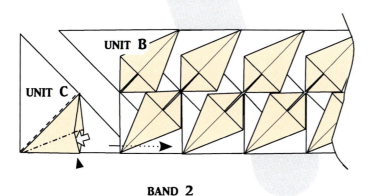

BAND 2

3. Add one more unit (UNIT C) to BAND 2 as shown and squash-fold the unused front pocket of UNIT C.

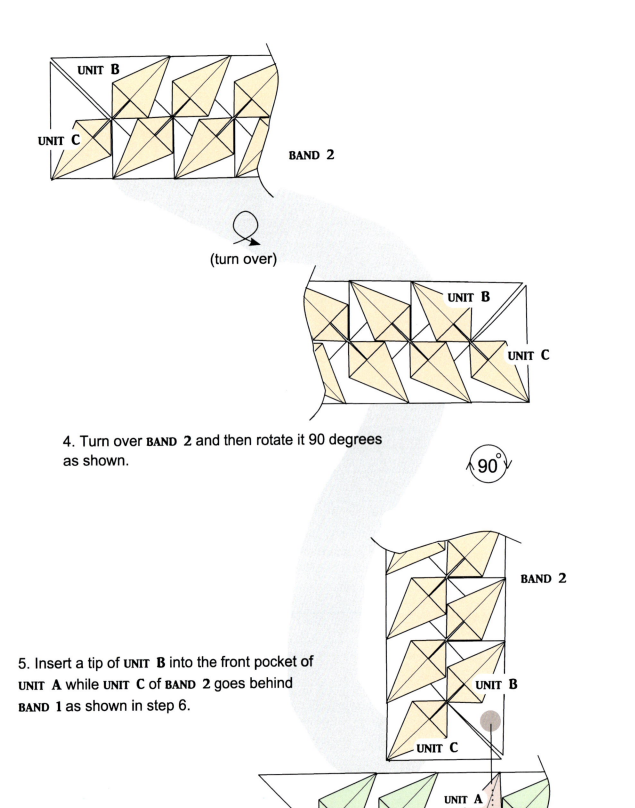

4. Turn over BAND 2 and then rotate it 90 degrees as shown.

5. Insert a tip of UNIT B into the front pocket of UNIT A while UNIT C of BAND 2 goes behind BAND 1 as shown in step 6.

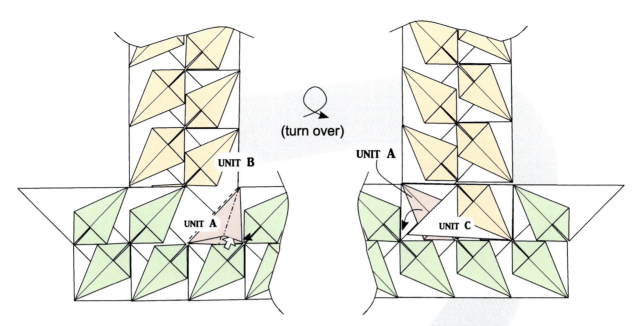

6. Squash-fold the pocket flap of UNIT A. Turn the model over.

7. Unfold the pocket flap of UNIT A and insert the tip of UNIT C.

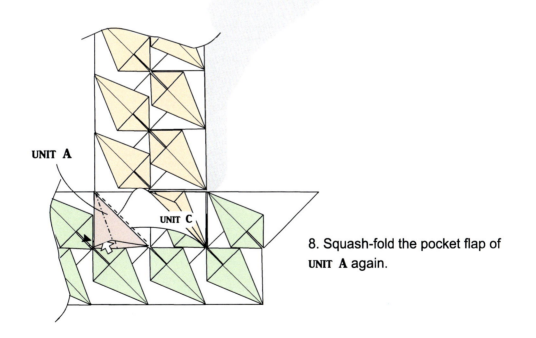

8. Squash-fold the pocket flap of UNIT A again.

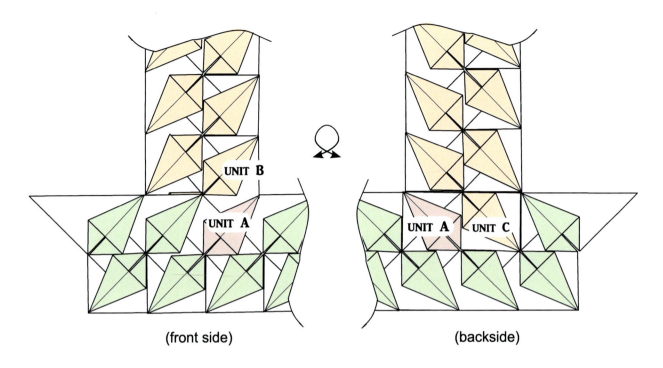

(front side)　　　　　　　　　(backside)

9. Two straight edge bands are perpendicularly connected.

PERPENDICULARLY CONNECTED DOUBLE RING

Double rings, single or multiple, like the ones below (simplified view) can be formed by this assembly. An example of a perpendicularly connected double ring is shown on the next page.
(Also see the photos on page 12 and 44.)

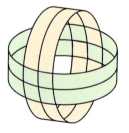
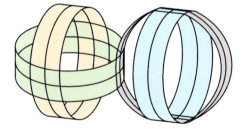

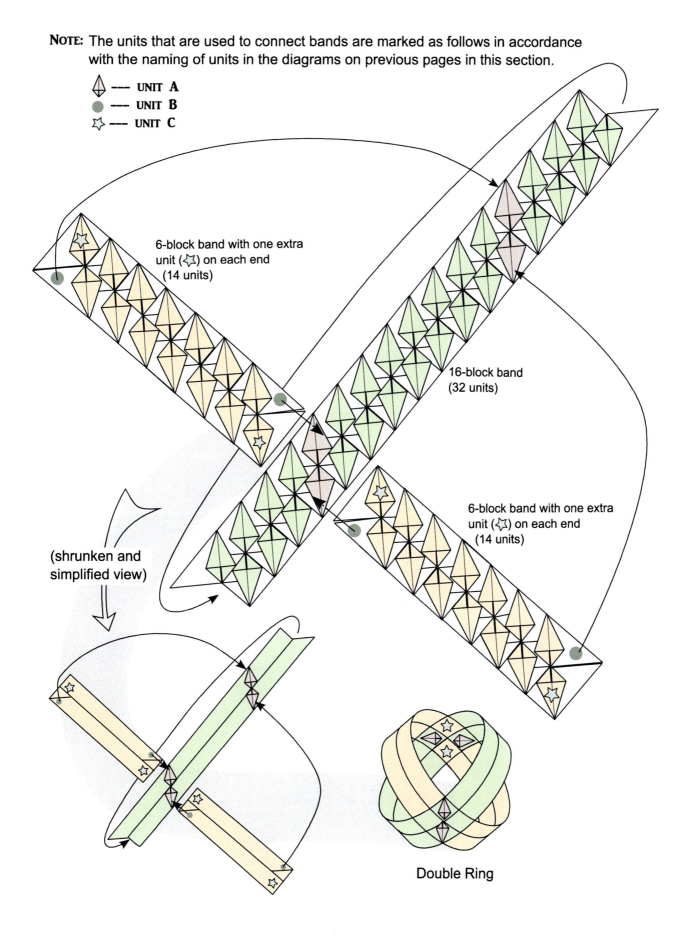

Double Ring

2.2 Angled Edge Assembly

Polygons (Single Layer Rings)

Two or more units can form a ring by connecting the last unit to the first unit. (Photos on pages 14-15)

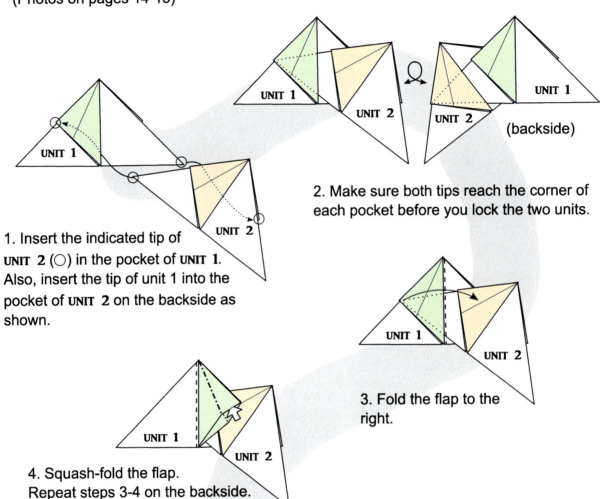

1. Insert the indicated tip of UNIT 2 (○) in the pocket of UNIT 1. Also, insert the tip of unit 1 into the pocket of UNIT 2 on the backside as shown.

2. Make sure both tips reach the corner of each pocket before you lock the two units.

3. Fold the flap to the right.

4. Squash-fold the flap. Repeat steps 3-4 on the backside.

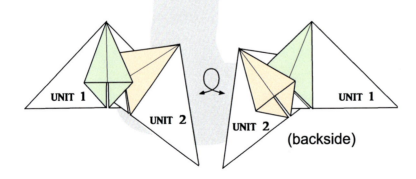

5. Two units are connected by two locks.

A. Forming a ring with two units

UNIT 2 is the last unit here.

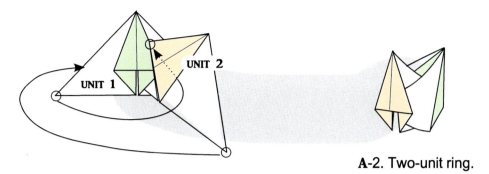

A-2. Two-unit ring.

A-1. Insert the tips of UNITS 1 and 2 into the others' pockets and lock in the same manner as above.

B. Forming a ring with three or more units

A decagon, a ten-unit ring, is shown here as an example. The ten unit ring lies flat because the angle between the units is very close to 144 degrees.

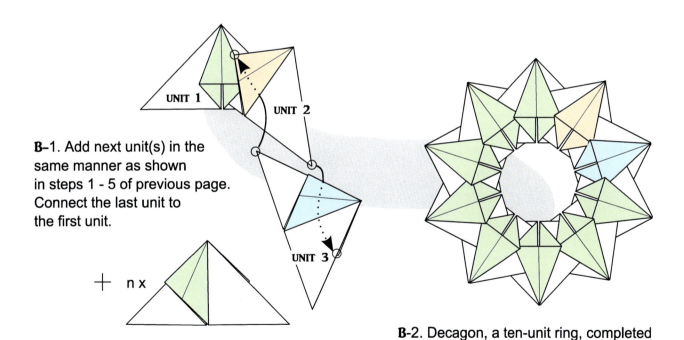

B-1. Add next unit(s) in the same manner as shown in steps 1 - 5 of previous page. Connect the last unit to the first unit.

B-2. Decagon, a ten-unit ring, completed (See photos on pages 14-15 for the rings with other numbers of units.)

> **NOTE:** In the assembly of these rings, it is also possible to use pockets on either side of a unit as was discussed in the earlier sections.
> One example is shown here. (Color of insertion flaps are changed alternately to make the difference more visible.)

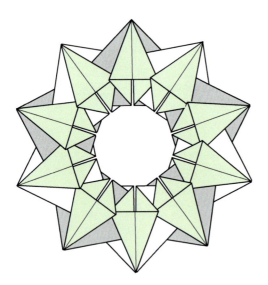

B-2a. Ten unit ring obtained in step B-2 of previous page

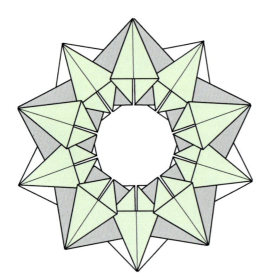

B-2b. A ten-unit ring assembled using pockets differently.

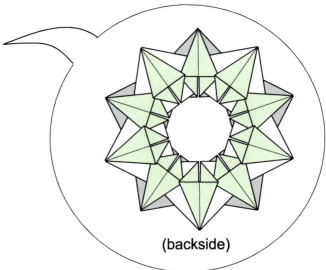

(backside)

10-unit rings formed with 5 x 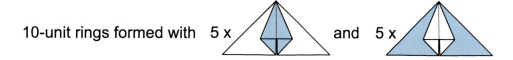 and 5 x

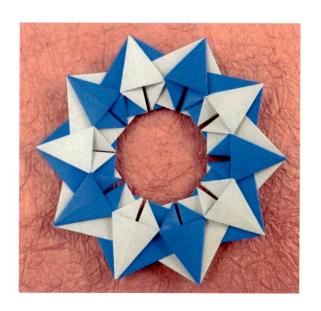

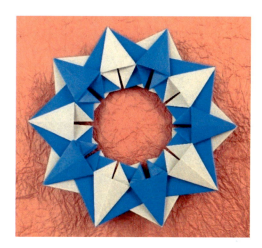

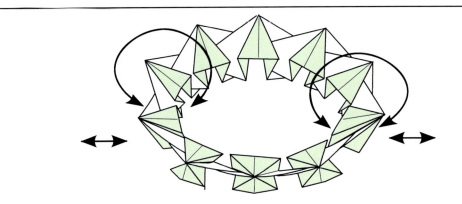

Rings with five or more units can be very flexible. Units are connected with strong double-lock joints on both sides of the ring, so the ring can be stretched and twisted around.

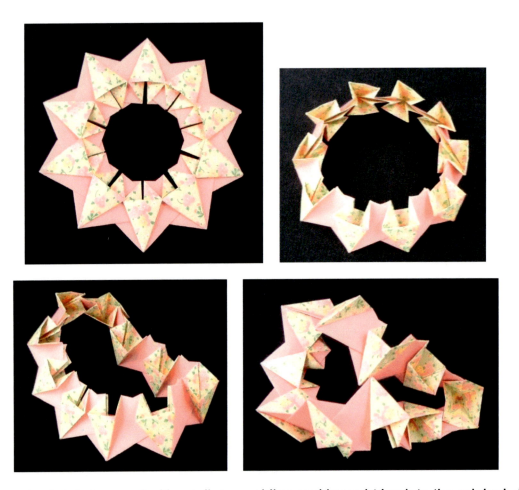

A ring can be twisted around without disassembling and brought back to the original shape.

POLYHEDRONS

(Photos on page 13)

DODECAHEDRON 1

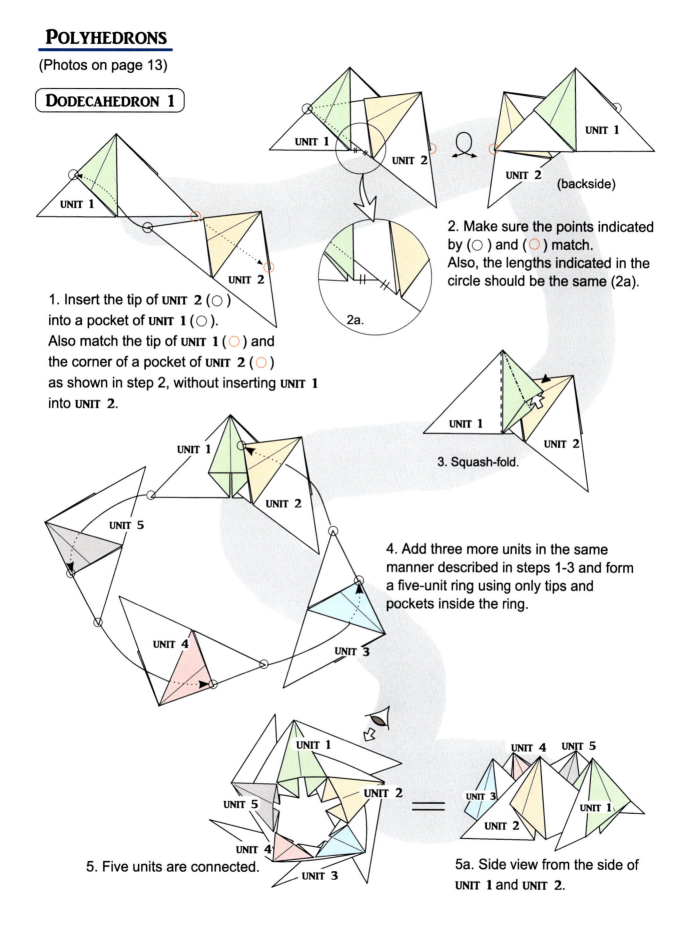

1. Insert the tip of UNIT 2 (○) into a pocket of UNIT 1 (○). Also match the tip of UNIT 1 (○) and the corner of a pocket of UNIT 2 (○) as shown in step 2, without inserting UNIT 1 into UNIT 2.

2. Make sure the points indicated by (○) and (○) match. Also, the lengths indicated in the circle should be the same (2a).

3. Squash-fold.

4. Add three more units in the same manner described in steps 1-3 and form a five-unit ring using only tips and pockets inside the ring.

5. Five units are connected.

5a. Side view from the side of UNIT 1 and UNIT 2.

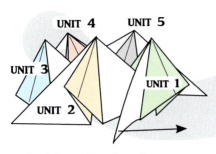

6. Move the tip of UNIT 1 to the right.

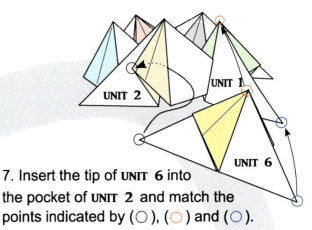

7. Insert the tip of UNIT 6 into the pocket of UNIT 2 and match the points indicated by (○), (○) and (○).

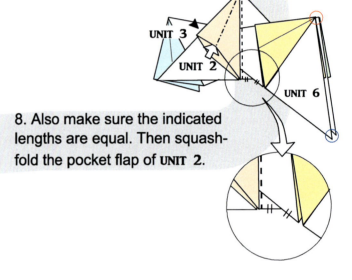

8. Also make sure the indicated lengths are equal. Then squash-fold the pocket flap of UNIT 2.

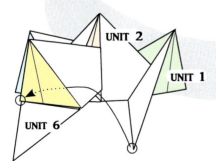

9. Move UNIT 6 to the left.

10. Insert the tip of UNIT 1 into the pocket of UNIT 6.

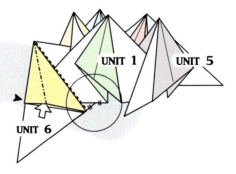

11. Make sure the indicated lengths are equal, then squash-fold the pocket flap of UNIT 6.

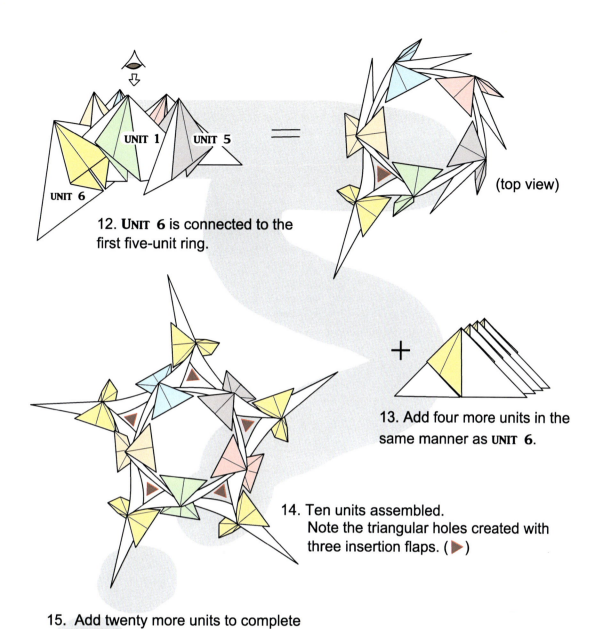

12. UNIT 6 is connected to the first five-unit ring.

(top view)

13. Add four more units in the same manner as UNIT 6.

14. Ten units assembled. Note the triangular holes created with three insertion flaps. (▶)

15. Add twenty more units to complete a dodecahedron 1.

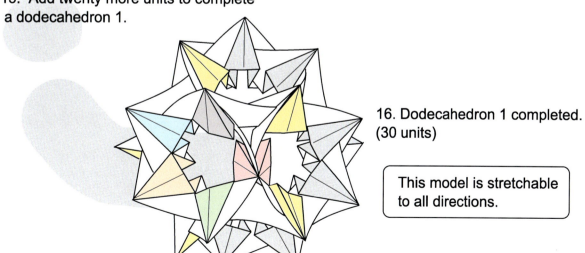

16. Dodecahedron 1 completed. (30 units)

This model is stretchable to all directions.

Dodecahedron 2 (Reverse Connection)

NOTE: Rings formed with insertion flaps are called "holes" here. Holes in Dodecahedron 1 are triangles while holes in Dodecahedron 2 are pentagons.

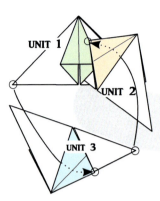

1. Form a three unit-ring in the same manner shown in steps 1 - 3 of Dodecahedron 1 on page 55.

NOTE: Reference points for assembly are the same as in Dodecahedron 1.

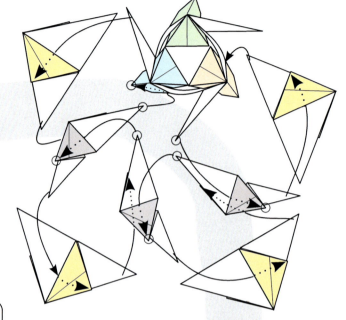

2. Add units so that five of the three-unit rings make a pentagon hole (⬠) as shown in step 3.

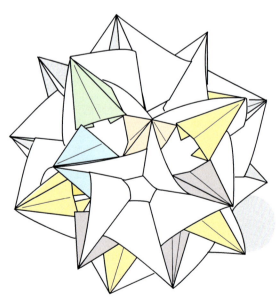

4. Dodecahedron 2 completed. (30 units)

3. Ten units are assembled. Add twenty more units to complete Dodecahedron 2.

Polyhedrons with Larger Number of Units

You can form polyhedrons with larger number of units by Angled Edge Assembly, using the same reference points described in previous pages.
Photos of truncated icosahedron (90 units) are shown as examples below as well as on page 13.
Polyhedrons with larger number of units are very flexible and do not maintain their ball shapes unless smaller or stiffer paper is used.

Truncated icosahedrons (90 units)
(Left: 4.25 in. x 4.25 in. squares. Right: 1.5 in. 1.5 in. squares)

POLYHEDRONS WITH SMALLER NUMBER OF UNIT – LIMIT OF ANGLES

You can form polyhedrons with smaller number of units, but there is a limit in angles to allow the formation because of the shape of the unit.

Two 12-unit polyhedrons shown here can be formed by squeezing each unit as shown below after units are connected during assembly.

Reference points for connecting units are the same as other polyhedrons described in previous pages.

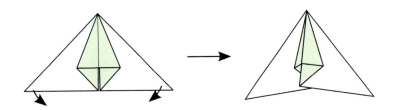

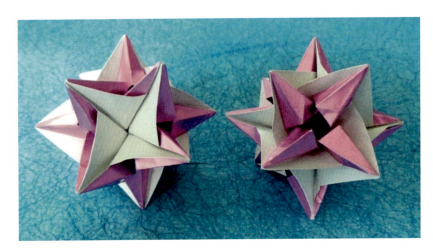

Two 12-unit regular polyhedrons (2.5 in. x 2.5 in. squares)

Twelve-Unit Polyhedron 1

Although it might not look like an octahedron, this model has a feature of octahedron. You can form this model by placing one unit on each edge of octahedron on the right. It has eight of 3-unit rings and six of 4-sided holes.

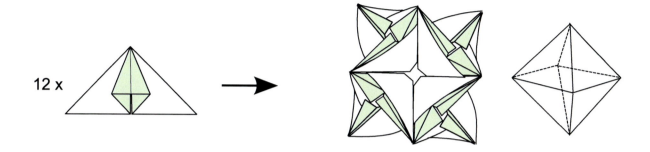

Twelve-Unit Polyhedron 2

You can form this model by placing one unit on each edge of a cube on the right. It has six of 4-unit rings and eight of 3-sided holes.

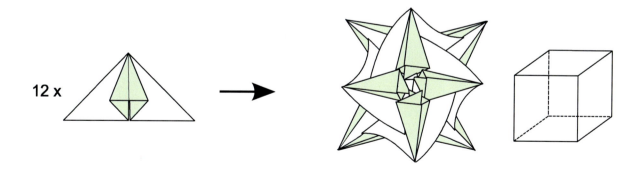

Tube (Layered Rings)

You need 10n units to form a tube (10 units for each layer).
Photo on page 11 has 800 units (80 layers).

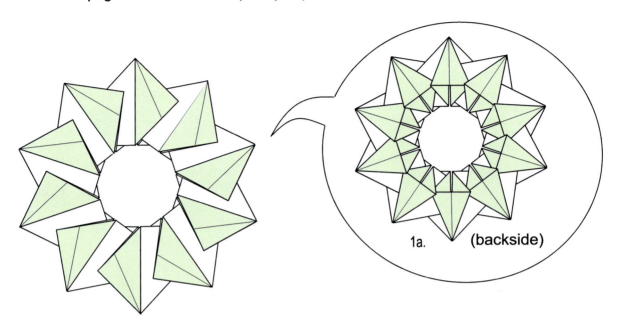

1. Form a ten-unit ring for the first layer as described in section B of page 51. But, while all pocket flaps on the backside are squash-folded (1a), pocket flaps on the front side are only folded to the right after insertion tips are inserted.

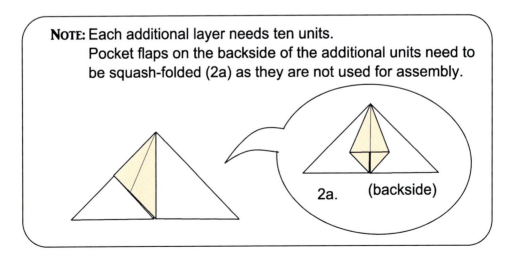

NOTE: Each additional layer needs ten units.
Pocket flaps on the backside of the additional units need to be squash-folded (2a) as they are not used for assembly.

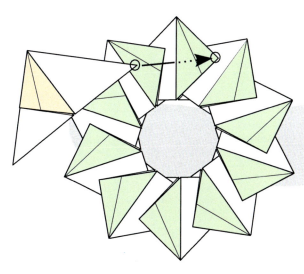

2. Insert a tip into a pocket of a unit on the first layer as shown.

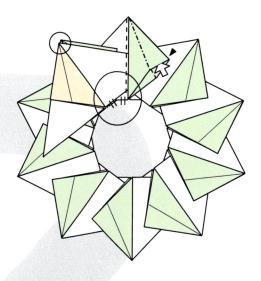

3. Make sure the indicated points are matched and lengths are equal. Then squash-fold the pocket flap to lock the units.

4. Add the second unit. One tip of this unit is inserted into a pocket of the first layer unit to right and the other tip is inserted into a pocket of the second layer unit to left.

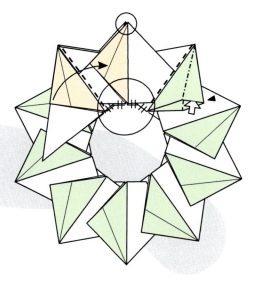

5. Note the matching points and the lengths.
Then lock the units as shown.

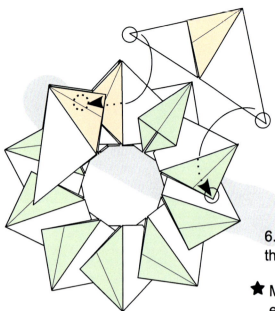

6. Keep adding additional units to complete the second layer.

★ Make sure reference points are matched every time.

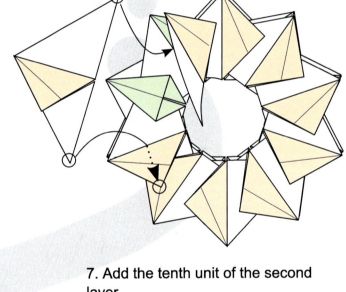

7. Add the tenth unit of the second layer.

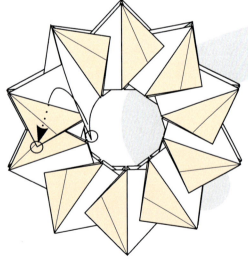

8. Insert the left tip of the first unit into the pocket of tenth unit. Then fold the pocket to lock.

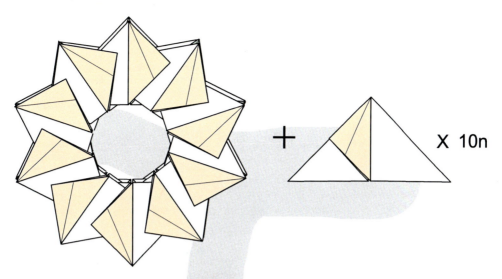

9. The second layer is completed. Add more layers in the same manner to form a tube of desired size. Squash-fold all the pocket flaps of the last layer.

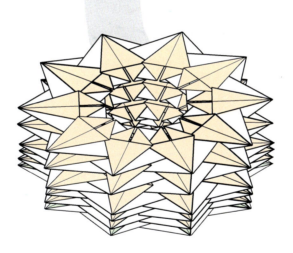

10. A tube completed.
This tube is highly flexible and can be stretched to all directions.

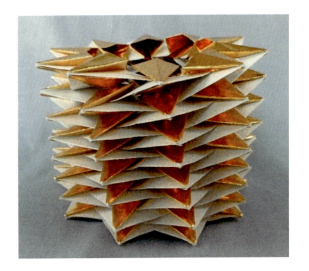

Top and side views of a tube (8 layers, 2.5 in. x 2.5 in. squares)

2.3 COMBINED ASSEMBLY

It is possible to join two or more modular pieces that are assembled using different methods.

PENDANT

This is one example obtained by combined assembly.

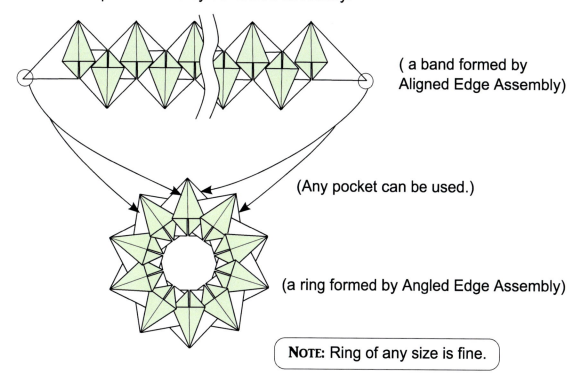

(a band formed by Aligned Edge Assembly)

(Any pocket can be used.)

(a ring formed by Angled Edge Assembly)

NOTE: Ring of any size is fine.

See photo on page 12.

NET TYPE MODULAR

Net type modular can be formed both by Aligned Edge Assembly and Angled Edge Assembly. Since nets assembled by the two different methods can be combined to form an object, I included both assemblies in this section.
While nets formed by Aligned Edge Assembly spread horizontally, nets formed by Angled Edge Assembly curve and can be used to form shapes like a torus.

NOTE: Use of foil paper is recommended for these models because foil paper helps the model maintain its shape better and makes assembly easier.

Net Formed by Aligned Edge Assembly

Net with 4-Unit Rings and 4-sided holes

The assembly of a net with 4-unit rings and 4-sided holes is shown here as an example.

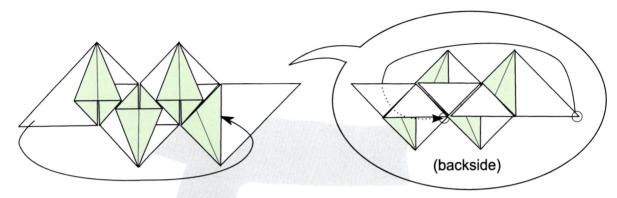

(backside)

1. Form a zigzag edge band (page 30) with four units by connecting only front side joints and connect the fourth unit to the first unit to make a ring that is joined with only inside joints as shown in step 2.

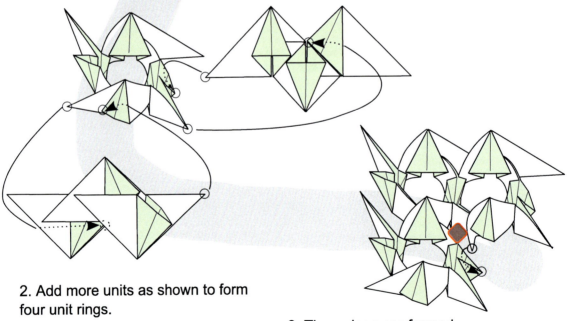

2. Add more units as shown to form four unit rings.

3. Three rings are formed, Insert the indicated insertion flap into the pocket to form a four sided hole (◆) with four insertion tips.

In order to simplify the view, the following symbols are used in this section to demonstrate the top view of the rings and holes formed with pocket flaps and insertion tips.

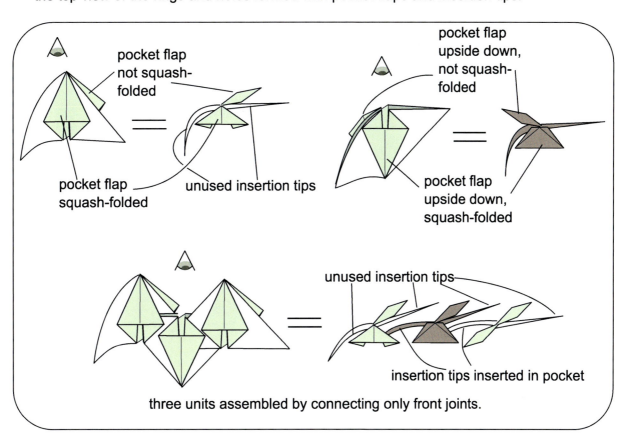

Simplified views of steps 2 and 3 of the previous page are demonstrated as 2a and 3a below by using the symbols above,

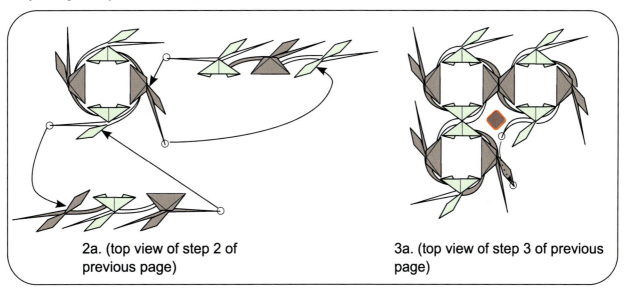

2a. (top view of step 2 of previous page)

3a. (top view of step 3 of previous page)

4. Add more units to form a net of desired size.
Note that all holes are four-sided.

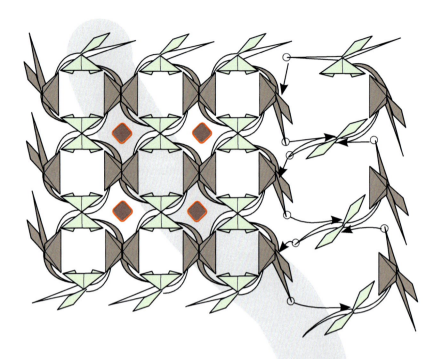

This net spreads horizontally.

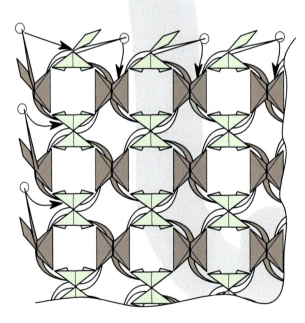

5. To complete a horizontal net, insert all unused insertion tips to the adjacent pockets as shown and squash fold all unused pockets.

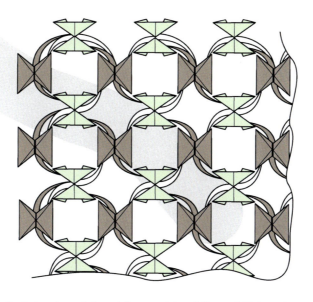

6. A horizontal net formed by Aligned Edge Assembly.
See photo on page 17.

NOTE: You can form a net with rings formed with other even number of units. Photo below shows a net formed with six-unit rings and four-sided holes.

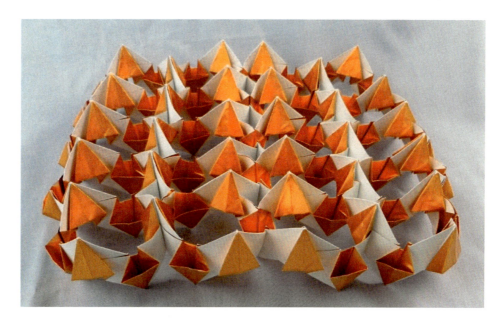

A net with 6-unit rings and 4-sided holes

You can form a cylinder by connecting one edge of a net to the other edge in either direction **A** (front of the net is the outside of the cylinder) or **B** (front of the net is inside of the cylinder) as shown in the simplified drawings on the right.

Cylinders formed by direction **A** and direction **B** have different appearances because orientation of each unit is opposite.

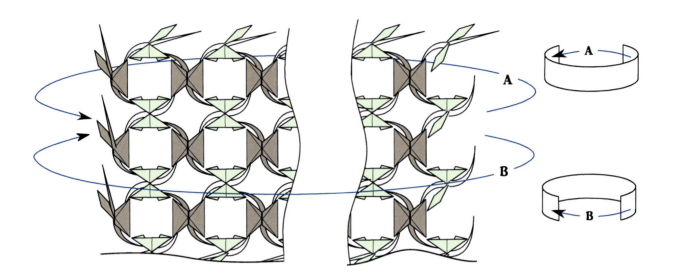

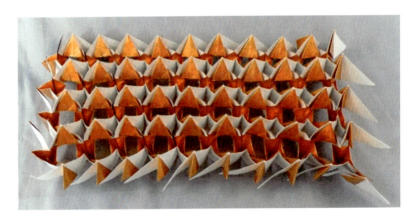

Front side of a net obtained above

Side and top views of a cylinder formed by direction **A**

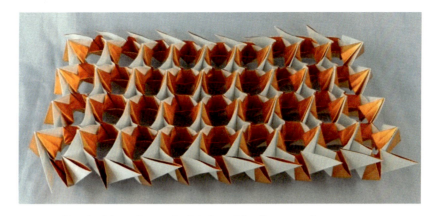

Backside of a net obtained in the previous page

Side and top views of a cylinder formed by direction **B**

A cylinder formed with a net obtained by Angled Edge Assembly (Pages 74-75)

Net Formed by Angled Edge Assembly
– Formation of Torus

A net formed by Angled Edge Assembly curves because of the angle of each joint. This feature can be used to form an object like a torus.

Net by Angled Edge Assembly

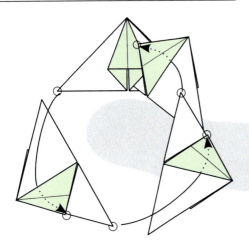

1. Form a four-unit ring by connecting only the joints on the front side. Reference points are the same as described on page 55.

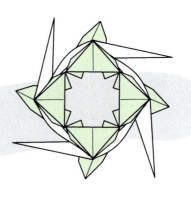

2. 4-unit ring. (top view)

In order to simplify the view, the symbols below are used to represent the top views of units in the diagrams in this section.

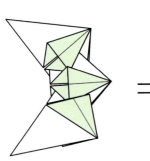

3 units connected by angled edge assembly with only the joints on one side connected.

non-squash-folded pocket flap

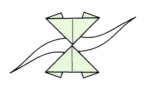

Top view of a unit with both flaps squash-folded.

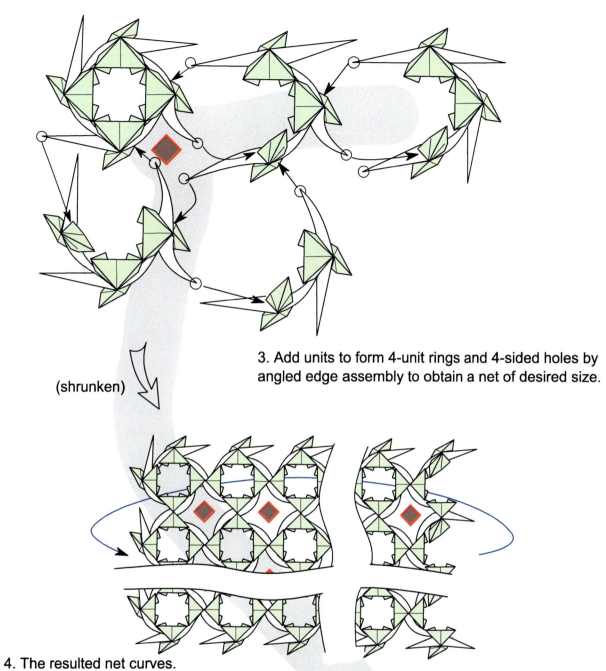

3. Add units to form 4-unit rings and 4-sided holes by angled edge assembly to obtain a net of desired size.

(shrunken)

4. The resulted net curves.
When you connect one edge to the other edge, it forms a curved cylinder as shown below.

5. A curved cylinder.

(approximate drawing of a curved cylinder obtained)

TORUS

A basic torus formed with Super Nobu Units has the following general properties and has a structure shown in Fig.1.

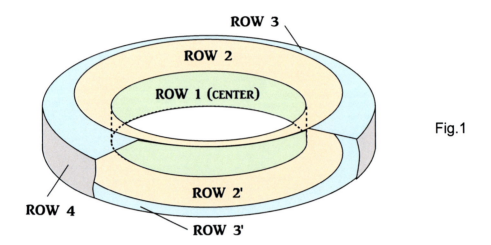

Fig.1

1. All rows of a basic torus consist of the same number of rings formed by Angled Edge Assembly but rings on the outer rows have more units to accommodate the greater circumference. When the number of rings in each row is "n," I call it "n-ring torus," e.g. a torus that has 10 rings in each row is a "10-ring torus."

2. Upper half and bottom half are symmetrical, i.e. ROW 2 and ROW 2' have the same structure, and so do ROW 3 and ROW 3'.

3. ROW 1 is the center circle and ROW 4 is the outer-most row that bridges ROW 3 and ROW 3'.

4. All units on the borders of rows are shared by two rows.

5. When the number of the rings in each row (n) is 10 or more, the numbers of units required in each row are: 3 x n for row 1, 2 x n for each of ROW 2 and ROW 2', 3 x n for each of ROW 3 and ROW 3', and 1 x n for ROW 4.

6. When the number of rings in each row is smaller than 10, ROW 2 and ROW 2' may need additional units to avoid overstretching each unit.

Photos of 12-ring torus and 9-ring torus are shown on the next page. (Note the additional units on the row 2 (red units) of the 9-ring torus.)
The torus diagrammed as an example in the following pages has 12 rings in each row.

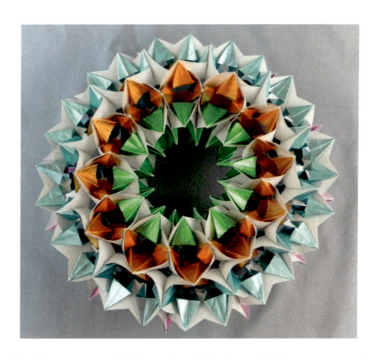

12-Ring torus (168 units. 2.5 in. x 2.5 in. squares)

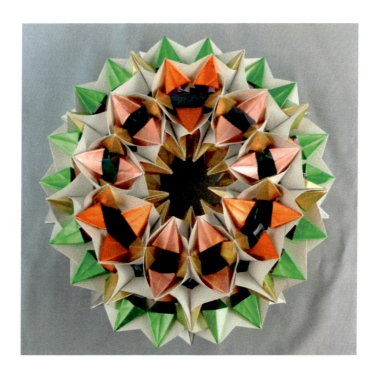

9-Ring torus (132 units. 2.5 in. x 2.5 in. squares)

FORMATION OF 12-RING TORUS (TORUS WITH 12-RING ROWS)

This torus requires 168 units. (3 x 12 units for row 1, 2 x 12 units for each of row 2 and row 2', 3 x 12 units for each of row 3 and row 3' and 1 x 12 units for row 4,)

Row 1 (36 units)

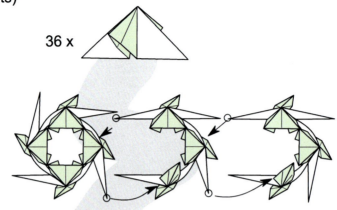

36 x

1. Form a 4-unit ring by Angled Edge Assembly as shown on page 55. Add units to form a chain of 4-unit rings as follows.

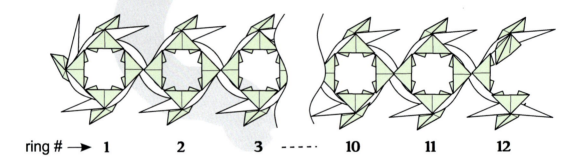

ring # → 1   2   3 ----- 10   11   12

2. This is ROW 1 before two ends are connected.

NOTE: You can connect the two ends of ROW 1 first and then add ROWS 2 and 2' if you prefer.

Rows 2 and 2' (2 x 24 units)

2 x 24 units

NOTE: In step 3, in order to keep the diagrams simpler, ROWS 2 and 2' are added to ROW 1 before the model is made into a cylinder and turned inside out. But it is possible to form a cylinder after only ROW 1 and ROW 2 are formed and turn it inside out, then add ROW 2',

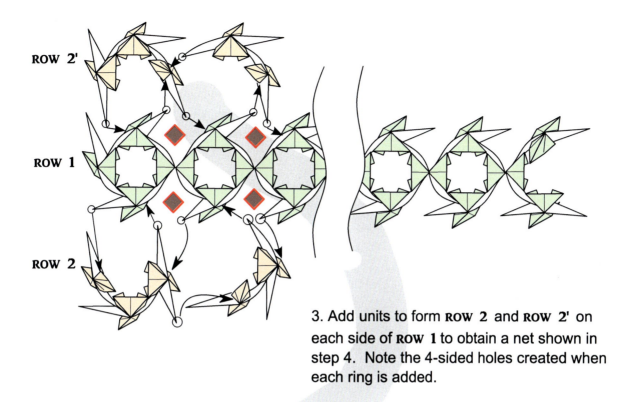

3. Add units to form ROW 2 and ROW 2' on each side of ROW 1 to obtain a net shown in step 4. Note the 4-sided holes created when each ring is added.

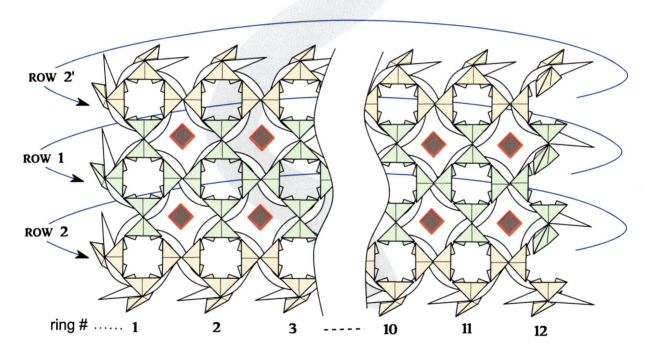

4. Connect the two short edges to form a short curved cylinder.

NOTE: Forming a net this way and then turn it inside out is easier than connecting two edges inside out.

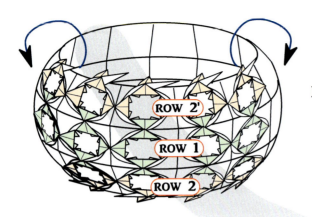

5. Carefully turn the cylinder inside out.

NOTE: This model is very flexible so it is easier to turn it inside out than it seems. But try to turn the whole edge evenly so that no joint or unit is overstretched.

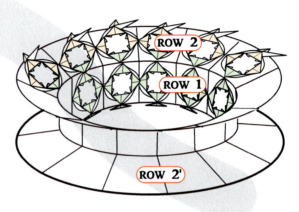

6. Inside-out cylinder. Top and bottom have the same structure.

NOTE: Drawings of steps 5 and 6 are approximate and do not include all the units.

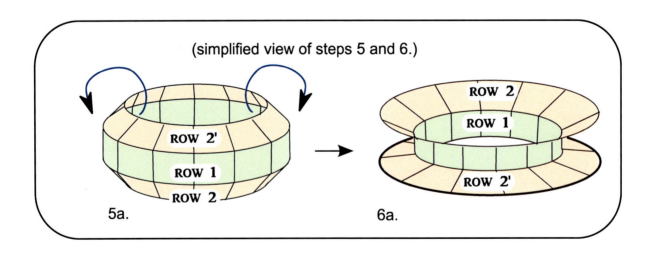

(simplified view of steps 5 and 6.)

5a.   6a.

6b.

(top and bottom views of 6a, the model obtained after steps 5-6.)
Top and bottom look the same.

ROWS 3 AND 3' (2 x 36 units)

Each of ROWS 3 and 3' consists of 5-unit rings.

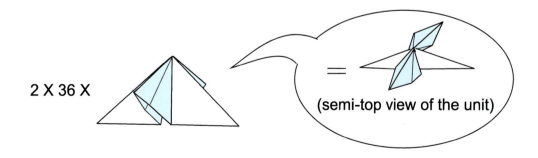

2 X 36 X

(semi-top view of the unit)

81

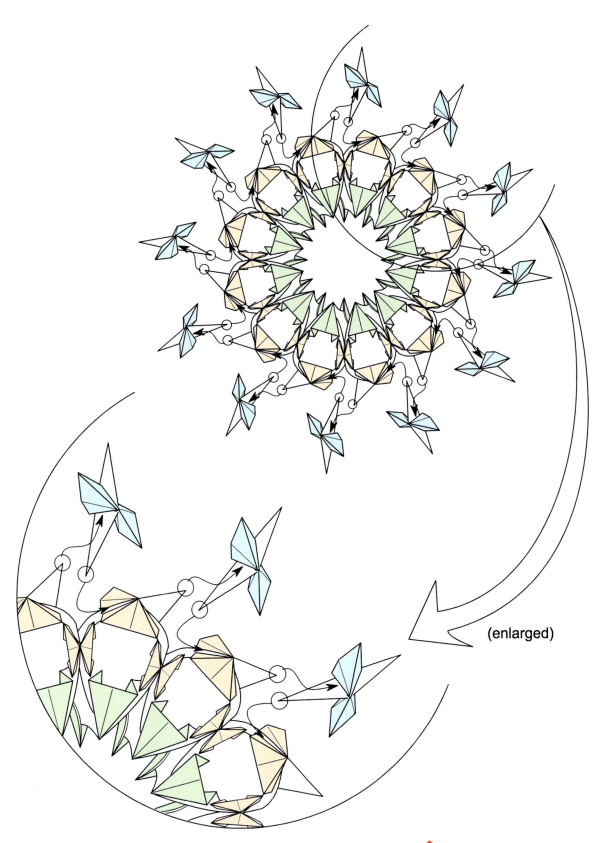

(enlarged)

7. Connect units to the edge of ROW 2 to form 4-sided holes (◆) as shown on the next page. Repeat the same on ROW 2' on the other end.

8. 12 units added to the edge of ROW 2, and to ROW 2' on the other end.

9. Form 24 of 2-unit blocks, 12 each for ROW 3 and ROW 3', that are connected on both sides.

(backside)

(shrunken view)

10. 2-unit block for ROW 3 and 3'.

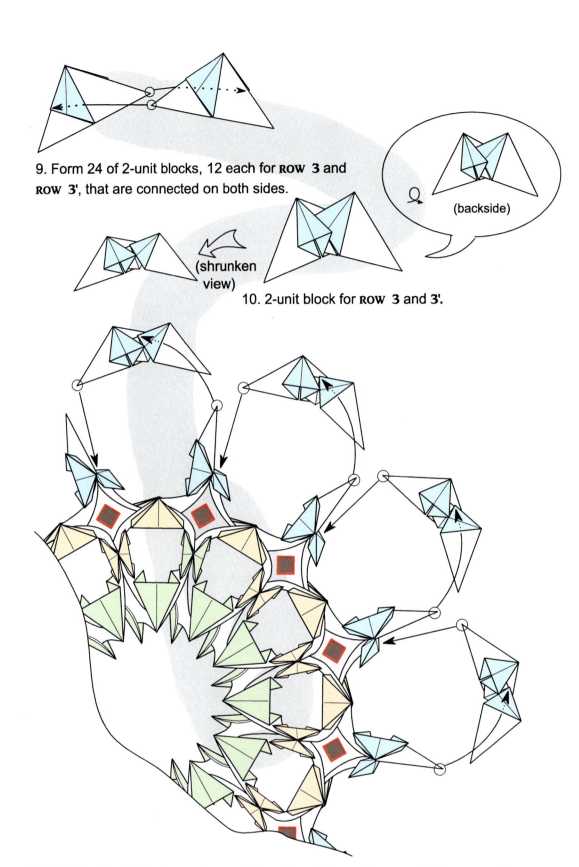

11. Add the 2-unit blocks as shown to form 5-unit rings all around to form ROW 3. Repeat the same to form ROW 3' on the other end of the model.

Row 4 (12 UNITS)

Row 4 consists of 6-unit rings. But in each of these 6 unit-ring, two units come from **row 3** and two more come from **row 3"**, so only 12 units are needed to form **row 4**.

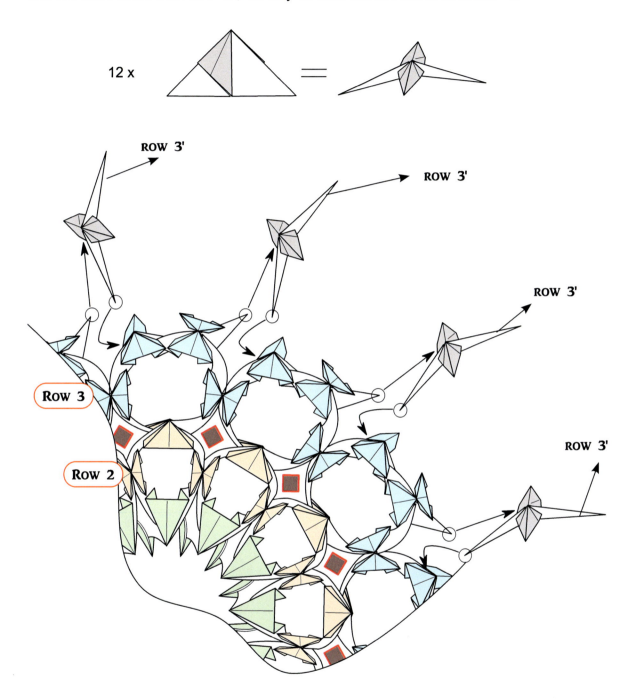

12. Add units to bridge **row 3** and **row 3'** to form 6-unit rings as shown in 12a and 13 in bird's eye views on the next page.

(forming ROW 4, bird's eye view)

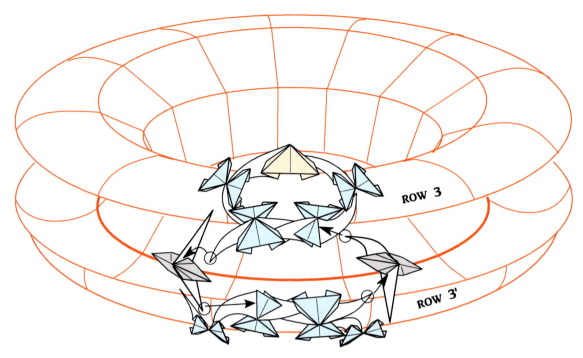

12a. Forming **ROW 4** by connecting **ROW 3** and **ROW 3'**.
Row 4 has twelve 6-unit rings.

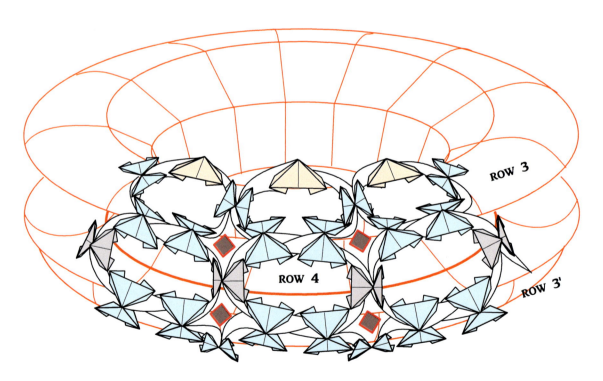

13. **Row** 3 and 3' are bridged to form **ROW 4**.
A basic torus completed. (Photos on pages 13 and 77)

VARIATION OF TORUS

You can form a taller torus by replacing **ROW 1** and **ROW 4** of a basic torus with a cylinder made of nets formed by aligned edge assembly, which is described earlier in this section (pages 68-73). **ROW 1** is replaced with a cylindrical net of 4-unit rings and 4-sided holes, while **ROW 4** needs to be replaced with a cylindrical net of 6-unit rings and 4-sided holes.

A cylinder that replaces **ROW 1** has to be formed by direction **A** described on page 72. (Compare the top view of a tall torus below and that of a basic torus on page 77.)

A tall torus below (also on page 17) can be obtained by replacing **ROW 1** of a basic torus by a net of 4-unit rings/4-sided holes (12 x 4 rings) and **ROW 4** by a net of 6-unit rings/4-sided holes (12 x 3 rings). You may use a net of 12 x 4 rings for **ROW 4**, but a 12 x 3 net fits well because it stretches and the whole model is flexible.

You can change the height of a torus by changing the size of the nets used.

Top view of a tall torus

2.4 OTHER ASSEMBLIES AND MISCELLANEOUS SUBJECTS

In previous sections, the assemblies of this unit were discussed in two major categories and the combination of the two. In this section, I will further explore the unique features of this unit described in the Unit section and try unconventional, less restrictive assemblies as well as limit of the joint.

As was demonstrated in the Unit section, an insertion tip of one unit can be inserted into a pocket of another unit with any angle within 45 degrees and the two units can be locked in the position by the two creases created by squash-folding the pocket flap. (Fig. 2a-2d and Fig. 3 on pages 23-24) This feature enable a unit to connect to other units of any sizes with any angle within certain range as if they are glued together.

ASSEMBLING UNITS OF DIFFERENT SIZES

Assembling units of different sizes is not new in modular origami, but there usually is a limit in size differences of the two units to be connected. With Super Nobu Unit, two units of any sizes can be connected by forming at least one joint as shown in Fig. 1 below.

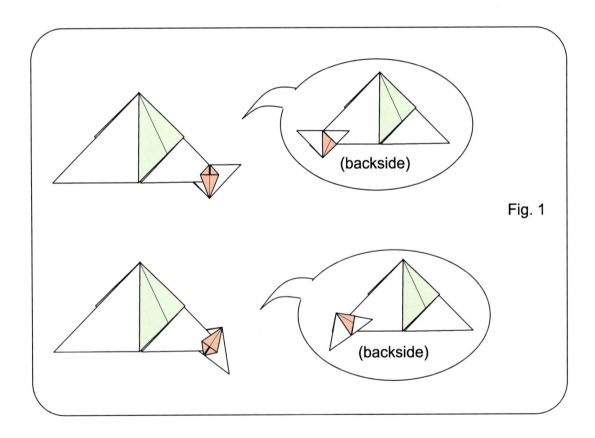

Fig. 1

As was seen in previous sections, two or more units can be connected to one unit.

If you use a different part of a pocket, other types of connections are possible. Some examples are shown in Fig. 2.

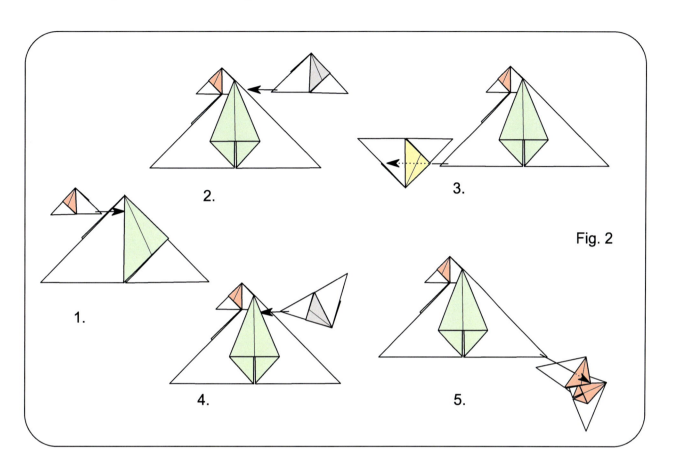

Fig. 2

You can connect them in any way you want!

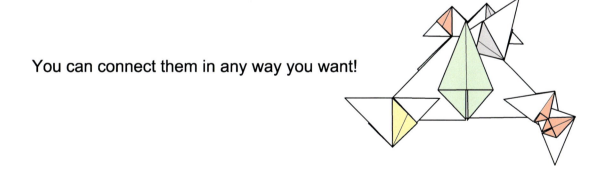

NOTE: One pocket can take more than one inserting tip. But inserting too many tips into one pocket makes the joint loose because of paper thickness.

HORIZONTALLY JOINED RINGS

Here, horizontally connected 10-unit rings are shown as examples. (Photos on pages 15-16)

NOTE: You can join any number of rings.
   The sizes of the rings can be the same or different.
   The two rings share one unit, so when you connect two 10-unit rings, second ring needs only 9 units.
   Pockets on either side can be used for this connection but you need to determine the inserting angle so that the finished model lies flat.

A. Two rings of the same size

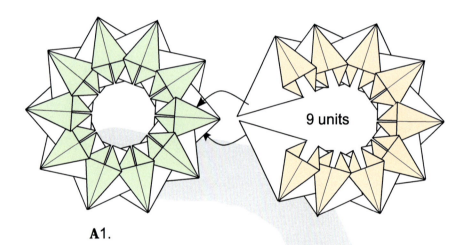

A1.

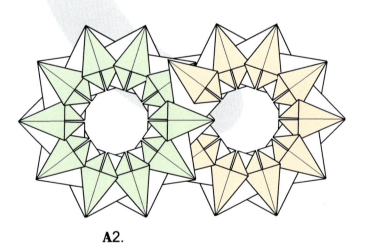

A2.

B. Two rings of different sizes

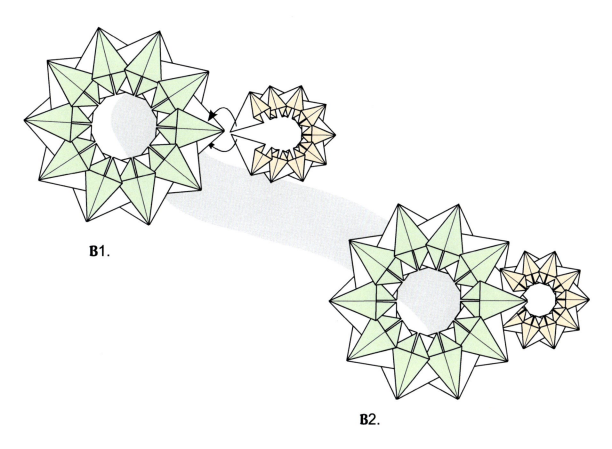

B1.

B2.

NOTE: Examples of joined rings with other numbers of units are shown in photos on pages 16 and 94.)

LOCKING UNITS OF DIFFERENT SIZES ON BOTH SIDES

When locking two units on both sides, insertion tips of both units need to reach the pocket of the other unit, and an insertion tip of the larger unit has to be inserted into a pocket of the smaller unit first to determine the position. Insertion tips of smaller units do not reach as deep in the pocket of larger unit as the units of the same size do, but still can be locked by at least one crease, or two creases when the size difference of the two units are smaller.
This is the same for both Aligned Edge and Angled Edge Assemblies.
(Photos of examples are on page 94.)

Aligned Edge Assembly

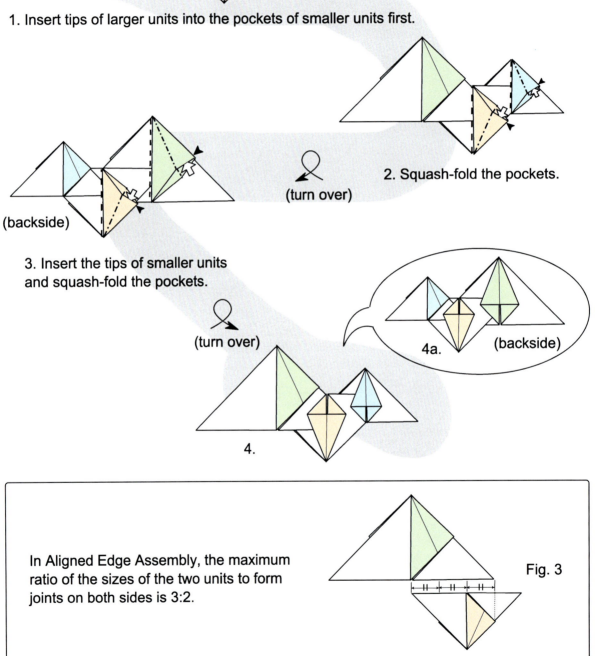

1. Insert tips of larger units into the pockets of smaller units first.

2. Squash-fold the pockets.

(turn over)

3. Insert the tips of smaller units and squash-fold the pockets.

(turn over)

4.

4a. (backside)

In Aligned Edge Assembly, the maximum ratio of the sizes of the two units to form joints on both sides is 3:2.

Fig. 3

Angled Edge Assembly

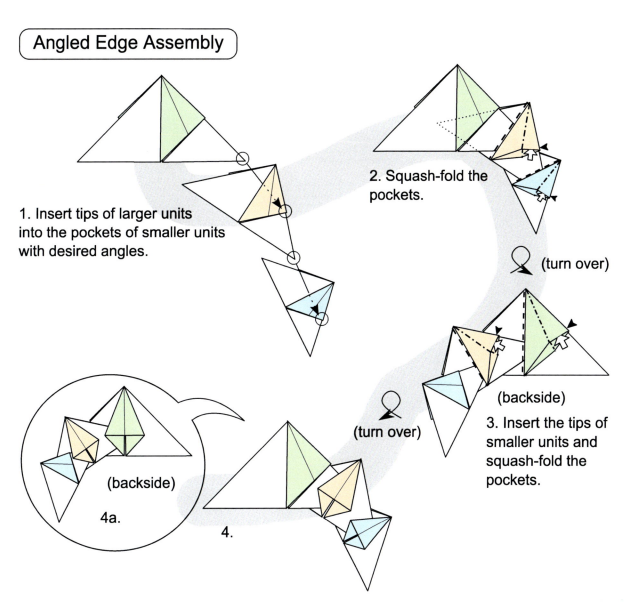

1. Insert tips of larger units into the pockets of smaller units with desired angles.

2. Squash-fold the pockets.

(turn over)

3. Insert the tips of smaller units and squash-fold the pockets.

(turn over)

4.

4a. (backside)

NOTE: Because you can connect units with any angle within 45 degrees in Angled Edge Assembly, you need to determine the angles of each joint depending on the final model you are planning to make.
See photos of examples on pages 16 and 94.

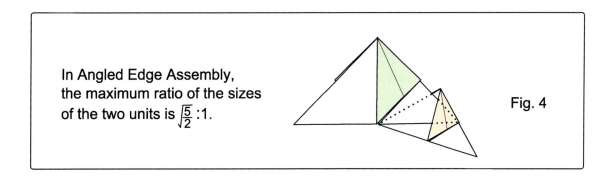

In Angled Edge Assembly, the maximum ratio of the sizes of the two units is $\sqrt{\frac{5}{2}}:1$.

Fig. 4

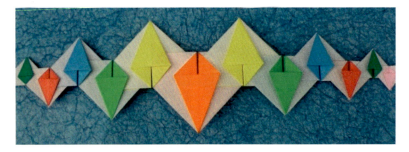

A band formed with units of different sizes (4, 3.5, 3, 2.5, 2, 1.5, 1.25 in. squares)

A ring formed with units of different sizes (4, 3.5, 3, 2.5, 2, 1.5, 1.25 in. squares)

Joined rings (5-unit ring made of 5 in. x 5 in. squares and 6-unit ring made of 1.5 in. x 1.5 in. squares)

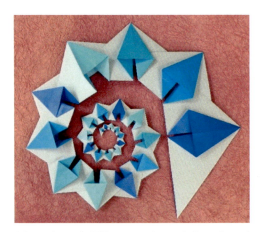

26 units of different sizes joined on both sides (The largest is 9.5 in. x 9.5 in. and the size of units is reduced by 10% continuously.) (Photo also on page 16)

Bringing Two Units Closer to Form Joints on Both Sides

Although there are limits in size ratios in both assemblies in order to form joints on both sides as mentioned in the previous pages, you can bring the two units closer by folding the tip of an insertion tip of the larger unit as if cutting off the tip by scissors.
This procedure works for both Aligned Edge and Angled Edge Assemblies.

Aligned Edge Assembly

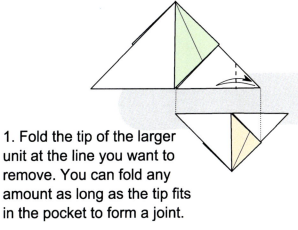

1. Fold the tip of the larger unit at the line you want to remove. You can fold any amount as long as the tip fits in the pocket to form a joint.

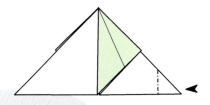

2. Inside reverse fold the tip.

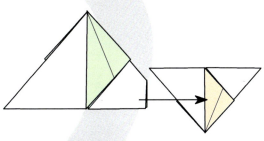

3. Insert the folded tip in a pocket of the smaller unit.

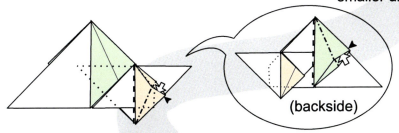

4. Squash-fold the pockets as shown.

5. The two units can be locked on both sides.

Angled Edge Assembly

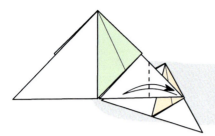

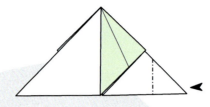

1. Fold the tip of the larger unit at the line you want to remove. You can fold any amount with any angle as long as the tip fits in the pocket to form a joint.

2. Inside reverse fold the tip.

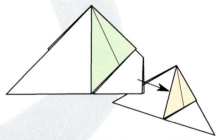

3. Insert the folded tip in a pocket of the smaller unit.

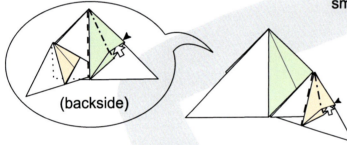

4. Squash-fold the pockets as shown.

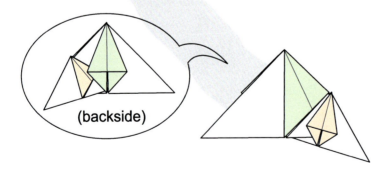

5. The two units can be locked on both sides.

DISASSEMBLING – LIMIT OF THE JOINT

As we have discussed in previous sections, the mobility of this unit and the strength of its joints allow us to stretch, turn, bend, and move around many of the models during assembly and after completion, but these joints are fairly easy to disassemble.

As was demonstrated in the Unit section, these joints are sets of simple pleats, i.e. an insertion tip is folded twice to form a Z shape after being inserted in a pocket.
A joint formed by Aligned Edge Assembly can be undone by simply pulling the two joined units to the opposite direction as shown in Fig. 5.
Joints formed by Angled Edge Assembly can be separated when two units are aligned and pulled apart as shown in Fig. 6.

In other words, this is the limit of these joints when you try to make certain shapes by stretching and bending a model. And, if you ever need to disassemble a model at some point, this is how it is done.

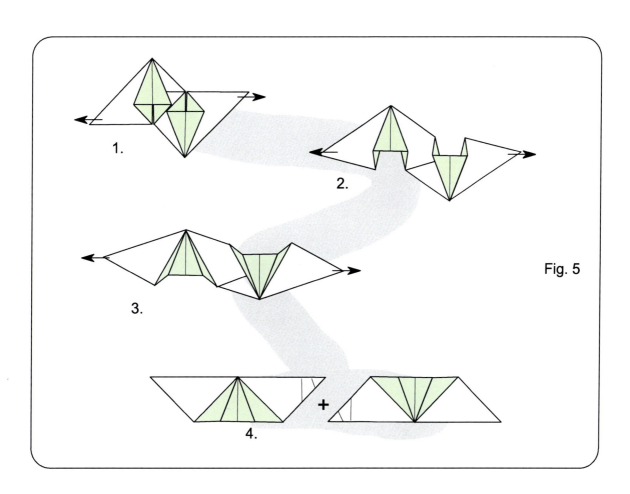

Fig. 5

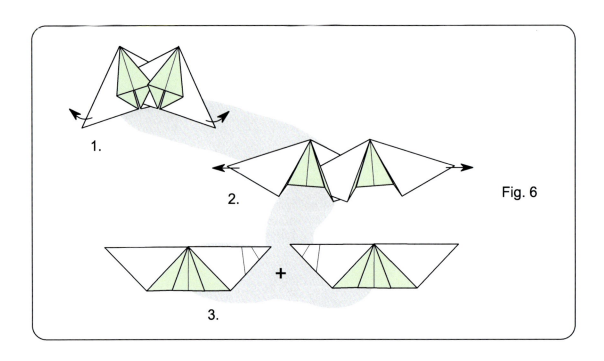

Fig. 6

  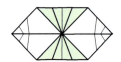

Well, this is the story of Super Nobu Unit.
Thank you for your interest!

About the Author

Born and raised in Tokyo, Japan, Nobuko Okabe first worked as an organic chemist in both her home country and the USA. She currently lives in New Jersey, USA and has been promoting origami by teaching people of all ages at local schools, libraries and various events.

Notes

Notes

Made in the USA
Lexington, KY
31 May 2018